Mallett & Son (Antiques) Ltd
141 New Bond Street London W1Y 0BS

MALLETT
Millennium

Mallett at Bourdon House Ltd
2 Davies Street London W1Y 1LJ

MALLETT Millennium

Lanto Synge

Fine Antique Furniture and Works of Art

Hubert

All best wishes from

Lanto.

22nd June 2000

in association with

ANTIQUE COLLECTORS' CLUB

First published in Great Britain in 1999
in association with Antique Collectors' Club
by Mallett Plc
141 New Bond Street
London W1Y 0BS
Tel: ++ 44 (0) 20 7499 7411
Fax: ++ 44 (0) 20 7495 3179

email: antiques@mallett.co.uk
website: www.mallett.co.uk

A catalogue record of this book is available from the British Library.

ISBN 1 85149 329 8

Design by Trevor Gray

Printed in England by Balding + Mansell Ltd

1 (Frontispiece)
*An exceptionally fine mahogany bureau bookcase
of the Chippendale period. English, circa 1760.*

Dedicated to
Her Majesty Queen Elizabeth
the Queen Mother
with her gracious permission

The Queen Mother and Francis Egerton, 1981

I love all beauteous things,
    I seek and adore them;
God hath no better praise,
And man in his hasty days
    Is honoured for them.

I too will something make
    And joy in the making;
Altho' to-morrow it seem
Like the empty words of a dream
    Remembered on waking.

Robert Bridges

Contents

———

Fin de siècle

A T the end of the last century Walter E. Mallett wrote a book entitled *An Introduction to Old English Furniture* with drawings by H. M. Brock. The book showed 168 pieces with reasonably lengthy captions. It was produced at the same time as Percy McQuoid was writing the first of four great volumes of furniture history divided by the woods employed: oak, walnut, mahogany and satinwood. Mr Mallett referred his readers to this seminal work of furniture documentation for more detailed information.

It seems timely and appropriate to mark the beginning of a new millennium with another Mallett book, also a sequel to the book which I produced in 1991, which illustrated a number of highlights from our enormous archive of photographs. I now have an opportunity to review a full century of dealing in English furniture and to look back at the wide range of wonderful pieces which we have been lucky to exhibit and to sell to our clients.

While this volume encompasses most of the important aspects of the history of English furniture it should be used more as an anthology of interesting examples. I think only one person attempted to read my previous Mallett book from cover to cover. That was my aged aunt. Having ploughed through endless descriptions, she told me sweetly that she had finished reading it and was now going back to revise. The selection of furniture and objects shown here have been presented in groups to illustrate different angles of appreciation.

Mallett's have been in business since 1865 and though our records are not fully consistent, we do have some catalogues dating back to the 1920s and 1930s. Mr Walter Mallett's illustrations in his book are only line drawings but in recent times colour photography has developed to convey gloriously the nuances of colour, texture and even patination to some degree. Mallett's were always at the forefront of photography in marketing fine furniture and in the last few decades huge steps have been achieved towards perfecting a better representation of the finest items. Records

of furniture, detailed pictures of smaller aspects on each piece and views taken at different angles all add now to an almost virtual image. This new volume, as a companion to *Mallett's Great English Furniture* of 1991, gathers together a carefully chosen selection of outstanding pieces drawn from our archives. Since writing that earlier book I have been able to track down photographs of a number of interesting and lovely pieces that ought to be recorded permanently and deserve to be published for the purposes of general reference.

We are acutely aware how lucky we are in the antiques business, to be handling every day beautiful artefacts created by the genius, imagination, skill and craftsmanship of many generations long gone before us. Patronage, vision and creativity came together at many points to produce exquisite beauty and it is important that we pass on and keep alive the vitality of really beautiful artefacts, while we have trusteeship of them. I hope this volume will help in sharing the heritage that is ever growing and that should be cherished and enjoyed.

I am very grateful to many people for helping me to prepare this volume. Past and present colleagues have contributed greatly to the project in both ideas and small details. Paula Hunt has edited numerous Mallett catalogues and has compiled more detailed information about many of our finest pieces; readers are referred to these catalogues. Clive Bartlett has taken the majority of the photographs which are of course the backbone of this book. I am very grateful to him for all his skill and patience.

History of Mallett

Bond Street in London is one of the most famous shopping streets in the world but the Mallett building, opposite Sotheby's is more of an Aladdin's cave than might even be suspected. It has within it a constantly changing collection of decorative arts equal to that in many of the great country houses. As a living museum, where you can handle every item (and you are even encouraged to take them away with you!), it has no parallel. It is of course a business, an efficient and hard working fully listed public company but, commerce aside, it is in its own way an ongoing work of art. Without being too pretentious about it, we are immensely proud of this thriving organism and take great trouble in constantly trying to keep up to standard a beautiful showplace for fine antiques that resembles a grand home. A somewhat palatial display of luxurious treasures is part of the modestly theatrical lifestyle that business interests allow us to act out in terms of presentation. That is all part of the fun of it, a celebration in room assemblies and all things offering themselves in a 'beauty parade' for new homes in private collections, palaces and museums.

5

The Green Dining Room is furnished with a seven pedestal table and an interesting set of Italian painted and gilt chairs made in the English Hepplewhite form.

11

Mallett has changed considerably in size and scope since its foundation in 1865 by John Mallett (a jeweller and silversmith), at 36 Milsom Street, Bath in Somerset. His son, Walter Mallett, who had joined his father's business in the seventies or early eighties, quickly assumed complete control and today he is acknowledged as the real founder of the firm. It was he who expanded the stock to include old silver and furniture and who arranged for the purchase of the lease of the Octagon in Bath.

That remarkable building had originally, in 1767, been designed as a church by the architect Thomas Lightholder, whose specific brief was to produce a structure which would be warm, comfortable and well lit. The abbey in Bath was not considered a suitable place for worship by the fashionable class since it was crowded with too many ordinary folk and animals and was dirty, even muddy underfoot. The Octagon fulfilled all the smarter requirements, and it became the most fashionable church in Bath. Eminent and distinguished visitors made a point of engaging a pew for as long as they stayed in the town, hiring it at the same time as they hired their lodgings. The most expensive of these were like small rooms, each with its own fireplace and easy chairs. Between service and sermon, an interval was allowed during which footmen poked the fires and saw that their master and mistress were comfortable. The vaults of this building were let out to a wine merchant, which gave rise to verses by Anstey:

> Spirits above and spirits below,
> Spirits of Bliss and spirits of woe,
> The spirits above are spirits Divine
> The spirits below are spirits of wine.

Since the building was leasehold, it was never consecrated, so when it fell into disuse in the 1890s an opportunity arose for Mallett's to take it over with the minimum of difficulty. New showrooms were built on each side of the church, with workshops and storage in the basement. A gas engine was installed to drive the polishing lathes, work the lift, make the electric light and circulate air through every part of the building by means of a fan. With improvement in communications, express trains serviced the West Country to and from London and facilitated attendance at the spa, bringing much added interest and business to Mallett's at the Octagon. It soon became the foremost antique business in the West Country. It was from here that W. E. Mallett wrote his *Introduction to Old English Furniture* in about 1900.

In 1908 the Franco-British Exhibition was held at Earls Court in London and the firm took a stand there. This was such a successful venture that Walter Mallett decided to open a permanent shop in London, and he took a lease of premises at 40 New Bond Street.

On his death in 1930, the business passed to a consortium of six of his employees, who in 1937 decided to close the Octagon premises and move the whole business to London. Francis Mallett became chairman. He advanced the business considerably in every respect, and was noted as one of the foremost connoisseurs of his day. He was a keen collector of clocks, watches and Oriental ivories, and on his death he left a large part of his collection to the Ashmolean Museum at Oxford.

In 1955 Francis Egerton took over the chairmanship, and it was from this date that Mallett's began to assume its present form. There was now no

6
A very unusual and rare large scale black lacquer bureau bookcase of the early eighteenth century.

7
*A view of a
showroom in the
former shop in
Bond Street,
including Indian
marble chairs.*

longer any direct family involvement in the company and, having brought
in two new directors, Francis Egerton was free to develop the business to
conform to his own exacting requirements. The hallmarks of his approach
were an insistence on the highest quality in every sphere, a meticulous
attention to detail and the deliberate projection of a highly personal,
decorative taste.

Shoppers in Bond Street became familiar with Mallett's façade at No. 40
with furniture displayed in its large curved windows on either side of the
door. Within, spacious showrooms on two floors displayed a very extensive

stock of furniture including mirrors, pictures and objects, each room carefully arranged to re-create the atmosphere of a private house. Two rooms were arranged as dining rooms, others as drawing rooms or reception rooms of a more general nature. A pine panelled library showed bookcases, desks and library tables and the downstairs rooms, also with period panelling, contained a fine collection of walnut and early eighteenth century furniture. A grotto, conceived on Italianate lines by Raymond Erith, with walls encrusted with shells, displayed small objects and glass.

From here, pieces travelled to museums and private collections all over the world. Mallett's are particularly proud of their close association with the major international museums. The Victoria & Albert Museum possesses more than fifty pieces of furniture which at one time or another formed part of our stock and many items have gone to American Museums.

Mallett at Bourdon House

Mallett's second business was established in 1961 at Bourdon House in the heart of Mayfair, until 1953 the London house of the late 2nd Duke of Westminster. Built for William Burdon Esq. in the years 1723–25, during the reign of George I, the house stood amidst fields and market gardens between the then emerging Berkeley and Hanover Squares.

In 1660, Mary, the daughter of Dr Doreson, rector of St Clements Dane, married Alexander Davies (hence Davies Street), a scrivener. He was a nephew of Sir Hugh Audley and inherited his estate. In 1677, their daughter, Mary, married Sir Thomas Grosvenor and thereby the property came into the family of the future Dukes of Westminster. Some fifty years later, the land was leased to the Burdons, who, shortly afterwards, started to build a house there.

Bourdon House still retains the character of a three hundred year old family home. Within its period setting there are three floors fitted with fascinating English and Continental furniture from nearly all periods but particularly from the eighteenth and early nineteenth centuries. In addition, there are objets d'art, decorative pictures, bibelots and amusing accessories. The stock is more eclectic than that at the shop in Bond Street; at Bourdon House masterpieces stand alongside the unusual and the exotic in a unique manner. The general taste combines unusual charm with quality of design and craftsmanship. The attractive paved courtyard provides a perfect background for antique garden statuary, ornaments and furniture, which form another exclusive feature of the business.

In 1983 Francis Egerton retired and shortly afterwards there was a management buy-out of the company under the leadership of Peter Maitland and David Nickerson. In 1987 Mallett Plc became a fully listed company on the London Stock Exchange with Peter Maitland as Group Chief Executive. In 1997 I succeeded him in that role with involvement in all aspects of the business and primary responsibility for the buying and the artistic management. Rex Cooper is non-executive Chairman and Laura Weinstock is also a non-executive director.

In May 1991, after eighty years at 40 New Bond Street, Mallett's moved to the present, larger premises at 141 New Bond Street, a few yards down the

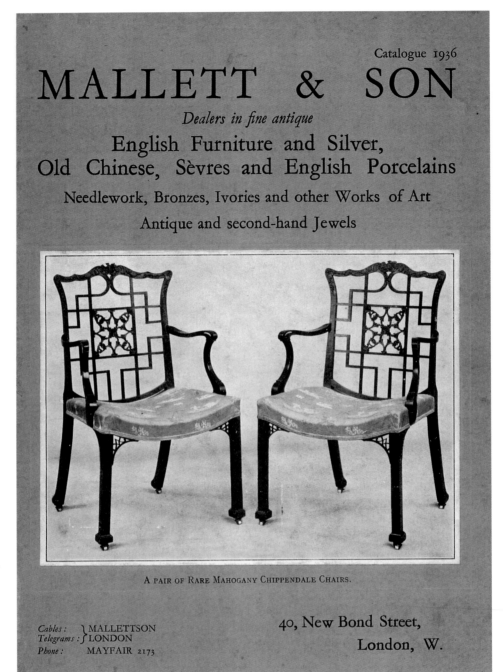

MALLETT & SON

Dealers in fine antique

English Furniture and Silver,
Old Chinese, Sèvres and English Porcelains

Needlework, Bronzes, Ivories and other Works of Art

Antique and second-hand Jewels

A PAIR OF RARE MAHOGANY CHIPPENDALE CHAIRS.

Cables : }MALLETTSON
Telegrams : }LONDON
Phone : MAYFAIR 2173

40, New Bond Street,
London, W.

8

The Mallett catalogue of 1936 shows two of a famous set of mahogany chairs made for Treworgey Manor, Cornwall, in the Chinese taste and incorporating the family crest (see fig. 269).

street and opposite Sotheby's. This move came as a result of the proposed redevelopment of the building at No. 40. However, the well known Mallett showrooms there have been partly preserved by a listing by the Department of the Environment with the support of English Heritage and other sympathetic organisations, as being of architectural importance. Rooms designed by the celebrated classical architect Raymond Erith in the 1960s, his last remaining shop interiors, are particularly noteworthy while in general most of the interiors were distinguished by interesting decorative features and finishes carefully devised by Francis Egerton and other members of the firm. Unfortunately some of these have inevitably been lost but a good many were adapted and used as a basis for the conversion and designs used in the new location.

Mallett's quickly became established in the fine building at 141 New Bond Street. Here we made some eighteen to twenty rooms on five floors displaying a tremendous variety of fine furniture in imaginative and none-too-strict period room settings ranging from walnut on the lowest floor through the main chapters of English furniture history: mahogany, giltwood, painted furniture, satinwood, the Regency and onwards. The premises include a special room for the antique glass department, whose range includes great early rarities from the seventeenth century to pieces from the twentieth century, for example a collection from the Whitefriars factory.

On the upper two floors the Mallett Gallery specialises in a wide range of paintings and watercolours. In 1988 we acquired the Christopher Wood Gallery, which specialised in nineteenth century pictures and works of art. Subsequently we decided to expand the picture department and over the last five years we have been developing this increasingly important part of the business and broadening the gallery's scope to include more seventeenth and eighteenth century paintings together with exceptional watercolours. These are shown in both the main galleries and also hanging in the furniture showrooms. The Gallery also holds regular exhibitions, including some of works by contemporary artists including Robin Bagot, Emma Tennant and Shân Egerton.

From its early days, Bourdon House was under the management of David Nickerson. It is now jointly managed by Thomas Woodham-Smith and Henry Neville who are also on the main board with those of us principally at the Bond Street shop: Paula Hunt, Peter Dixon, Giles Hutchinson Smith and myself. The two Associate Directors are John Smith, who runs the glass department, and James Harvey who is manager of the Gallery, while Richard Cave, Jeremy Garfield-Davies, Katie Pertwee, Felicity Jarrett and Tarquin Bilgen are also important team players.

9
This magnificent polygonal library table of about 1730 is monumental in form with gilt carving in the classical manner. It was sold by Mallett in 1930.
(See page 99.)

The several departments and numerous rooms in the two Mallett buildings are thus individually designed to display the finest English and continental furniture, together with decorative pieces, pictures and lamps and rare objects in what I hope are enviable settings. These rooms try to continue the Mallett tradition of combining high quality and individuality and exhibiting furniture with an eye to the overall decorative scheme, taking care that each piece complements its neighbour. It is part of Mallett's philosophy, that as well as the particular excellence of individual antique items, each piece should take its part in being carefully placed in the creation of a room. The making of interiors is in itself an art form, in which our clients can participate and which we can help provide.

Fine antiques should not only be a sound investment but also an embellishment and a pleasure in everyday life. This is an important aspect of our business.

I think I may be allowed to observe that the present state of the antiques business is at a remarkable level of professionalism. The high prices involved demand this and personally I feel confident that Mallett's, like other top specialists, operate on an unprecedentedly serious and respected level. The commitment of the directors is undoubted and each is a known expert in one or more fields. Above all the motivating objectives are not only a bread-winning operation but more importantly they are the cherished way of life of the family of friends who run and manage the business for all its purposes. Scholarship and boundless curiosity are part of the fascination that is behind the tireless research and preparation that goes into presenting fine things in a proper way. The results of such endeavours greatly increase the interest and delight of them. More and more, in-depth history, provenance and general background help to enforce and enhance the intrinsic character of many pieces. Obviously beautiful they may be, wonderfully conceived and made, a fine shape and colour, but if we can establish who designed them, possibly who made them, where, for whom and so forth, that all adds an extra dimension. In English furniture however these facts are usually not recorded. But even indications of design history, the background to the forms, the origins of historic fashions, the taste and influences of local patrons and craftsmen help to fill in an interesting picture. Sometimes we can establish the house for which a piece of furniture was made, even the room for which it was designed. These of course are interesting elements in biography. So also however, can be a piece's subsequent history and it can be fascinating to know aspects of its story as it passed from a period of neglect perhaps to re-evaluation and its place in collections in the eighteenth, nineteenth or twentieth centuries.

There is renewed respect for some of the best Edwardian and later collectors and writers, people such as our founder Mr Mallett, for Percy McQuoid, Herbert Cescinsky, R. W. Symonds and Ralph Edwards and also more recently Noel Terry, Irwin Untermyer and Samuel Messer, to name just a few. These renowned connoisseurs identified many fine objects as touchstones of quality. There are a number of similarly passionate devotees today who are building up important furniture collections and in the process they can themselves exercise a quintessential stamp of quality and approval. Jon Gerstenfeld for example has recently built up and published a remarkable collection. Some of these collections may remain intact and will survive, as some great houses, for almost ever; others will be divided and

10

A group of neo-classical furniture includes a magnificent commode attributed to Pierre Langlois and a pair of giltwood torchères perhaps designed by James Wyatt.

re-circulated again but in each case their inclusion in a collection can be of considerable interest in its own right. Not all the earlier collectors got it right and some were not well advised. Sometimes scholastic views and matters of taste seem to have changed beyond recognition. Great collectors of paintings and furniture around the turn of the last century seldom succeeded in both equally well. Paintings were more obvious, more easily recognisable. Furniture was considered a lesser adjunct and a good many museums have subsequently found themselves with some grand but dubiously authentic items below their splendid English pictures.

It is certainly true that far fewer errors of judgement are made today. Businesses such as Mallett's have to get it right. The sums involved are great, the competition is fierce and there is no room for inefficiency. There is no doubt that expertise has developed hugely over the last century. A glance at Mr Mallett's book, and others of the period, will show what now seem questionable judgements. Things have moved on a lot. We know so much more, investigate furniture much more thoroughly and have a great many more supporting facts available to use in making evaluations. It may be that in years to come there will be some sort of x-ray machine that will be able to see through veneers and gilding into every component of a piece of furniture, and will be able to identify each small piece of wood to a tree, dating it precisely! But excluding such sleuth, experts are now able to have a confident view of true authenticity, greatly superior to that of fifty years ago. Even in recent decades specialist experts have emerged with limited and highly in-depth knowledge of small and fascinating fields. Recently I called on a celebrated judge of Indian furniture made with ivory for Europeans, only to be told that another colleague knew even more about the work of a specific area, in this case Sri Lanka. Restorers are amongst some of the best and most experienced authorities, knowing as much as academics in terms of what lies behind the real history of a piece. Design is one thing but the facts of fate in the layers of ageing, repairing and restoring are altogether another.

Together, museum historians, trade experts and the practical workers in conservation and restoration have developed a scientific analysis alongside a general investigation into the true state of furniture and its history to a very high level. Mallett's have certainly played an important role in this growing field and I feel that we are fortunate to be around now that it is so well established.

Every age must remember its history anew: each generation sees things from a different perspective. One of the most absorbing long term interests to follow in a career in the antiques trade is observing and trying to read and forecast changes in judgement, taste and fashion. These are not necessarily incompatible though they often pretend to be mortal enemies. Each is tempered by trends and knowledge. What does remain fixed and permanent are true values but the assessment of these is as elusive as gold. Many will say that quintessential evaluation, just like taste and fashion, is only a matter of opinion. Weighing these is extremely dangerous and, to some extent has to remain subjective. But judgement must be made in the process of selection.

Nothing is more fraught than questions of taste; nothing is more fickle than fashion. Both are important in different ways and each flirts with so-called true values. In terms of furniture collecting there is no doubt that questions of taste are important but that they change, partly as a result of fashion but guided in theory by reason as opposed to mere whimsy of the times. When I came to Mallett's in 1969 'old fashioned taste' was rather frowned upon. It was represented by heavily carved, rather dark (almost black) mahogany furniture, sometimes upholstered with old, somewhat faded and definitely dusty needlework, probably the original covering. These aspects were despised in favour of simpler lines, as in shapely, less carved cabriole legs, plainer veneered furniture, or pale satinwood and elegant painted furniture. While the latter are still admired we have since learned that the formerly rejected old fashioned pieces are often of superb quality, only needing careful cleaning and wax polishing and proper conservation of the needlework upholstery to be rejuvenated as just masterpieces. In those former times it was even known to take the tapestry or embroidered coverings off furniture in favour of a less complex upholstery material. Fashion has since taught us to like again a wide mix of patterns alongside each other and to see this as rich and exciting. Once again there is no problem with heavily ornamented designs where patterns are

11
This recent room setting shows in the foreground a large Chinese Imari fish bowl, a tapestry covered chair from Wentworth Castle (see also fig. 175) and a marble chimney-piece attributed to Isaac Ware, circa 1756.

sensitively balanced and devised to achieve great richness and layered elements of beauty. In less than thirty years what was seen as 'old fashioned taste' is not only acceptable now but stands at the pinnacle of both taste and fashion. There were very few who kept their nerve in the judgement of true value in those, admittedly extreme circumstances, and I cite that state of affairs to illustrate a tendency that had a significant effect in the art and antiques market, and as an example of changing views. Comparable in picture dealing, must be the market evaluation and saleability of old master paintings that were so greatly undervalued in proportion to the absurd prices paid for second rank impressionist pictures.

Looking at early Mallett records, photographs and catalogues, we notice that oak furniture features a great deal, and with high prices. Much of that now seems out of proportion and we know that some of it was not what we would now consider good enough. Inevitably oak furniture was often in the form of built-in fixtures in houses and so was removed and adapted to become separate standing pieces. Many other alterations were made to rare surviving elements to make them a useful and practical size. On a recent conference with the Furniture History Society, I was with a group of experts for several days but we were amazed how few pieces we saw in a number of great houses that were in an original state.

Following the age of oak, the next wood period in the history of furniture is of course walnut. This field has had a different reputation. From the early part of this century walnut furniture has been consistently valued and always been in vogue. It has never fallen out of fashion and it is interesting to note that even in more recent periods of recession walnut furniture has held its own against weakening business trends. It is appealing in so many ways and almost everybody enjoys its neat proportions, varieties in veneering, colour and character.

Other fields and periods have moved slightly in and out of favour, often with little justification. I have already alluded to certain heavily carved mahogany furniture. Satinwood has had good and bad fluxes but is of course, at its best, quintessential of Georgian cabinet making, considered probably the best ever achieved, so must be a 'blue chip' in true value. Painted furniture is to my mind amongst the most beautiful that England ever produced and it is curious that while it is still considered to be in good taste by 'those who know' it is not currently fashionable. It is important that its condition should be good (as with all furniture) and that the paint surface should be the original and that restoration should be minimal. For my money the finds in this field can be almost unequalled in beauty and often nowadays I feel that such pieces are undervalued aesthetically and commercially. That is the nearest I can give in terms of 'bargains' at present, but who is to know how taste and fashion will proceed in relation to the pursuit of ultimate true values. So much of all three has to be subjective.

12

The Great Room at Bourdon House was inaugurated in 1999 with an exhibition of glass furniture by Baccarat and Osler together with contemporary glass sculpture by Danny Lane.

The Late Seventeenth Century

⟨⟨⟨❖⟩⟩⟩

THE concepts of comfort and luxury were achieved in mediaeval and post mediaeval houses by a rich use of textiles but by the seventeenth century we see that furniture in more developed forms was much more lavishly shaped, decorated and upholstered. The old solid look of oak was replaced with more elaborate forms with lighter features, intricately carved, painted, gilded and hung with new expensive textiles. The new shapes contrasted, for the first time, mass with space – shapes formed with curves and pierced with carving made open frameworks emphasising delicate lines, though also with immensely grand ornament.

Emblematic of these achievements are a magnificent pair of painted and gilded armchairs probably from Quenby Hall, Lancashire (fig. 13). These are of beechwood and are painted black with some parts richly gilded. The use of turned legs with scrolled toes, curvaceous arms, the pierced cresting and the similar front stretcher, are all features of Northern Europe. The bold use of pilasters on the back, basic motifs of Italian Renaissance inspiration, are a sign of the maturity that had now reached across Europe, in furniture design. The chairs were acquired by Temple Newsam House, Yorkshire.

Another splendid chair (fig. 14), also of about 1680, is simpler in decoration, beautifully shaped and made to look welcoming and comfortable. In this case richness is achieved by the upholstery covering, a glorious cut velvet of wool, probably Flemish, made to an Italian design, in turn inspired by Byzantine and Ottoman patterns.

The exchange of international ideas in design was already a central aspect of richness by the second half of the seventeenth century and imports of exotic forms and materials, especially from the East were incorporated on many occasions. A table of circa 1680 (fig. 16) has turned ebonised legs in barley-twist (or salamonic) form, typical of Holland but the top and sides incorporate beautiful Indian inlaid ivory work in floral patterns familiar in Moghul workmanship of the sixteenth century. Whether the table was

13
Made in about 1700 these splendid William and Mary armchairs combine North European carved forms with pilasters on the backs, a classical feature from Renaissance Italy.

14
A luxurious late seventeenth century chair upholstered with costly cut velvet imported from Europe

entirely made in India for the European market or was made in Europe using Indian elements is open to conjecture.

Certainly English however, is a remarkable pair of brass andirons with enamel decoration (fig. 15) comparable to another pair at Ham House. They were almost certainly made by Daniel Dametrius and his partner Jacob Monomia who came from the continent in 1649 and set up a brass foundry in Esher, Surrey. Enamel decoration of this kind is exceedingly rare. It was an art that originated in China and of course was perfected in France and England in the Middle Ages. These andirons date from about 1660.

A charming marriage of Eastern and Western concepts is achieved in a dressing table and toilet mirror of the William and Mary period (fig. 17). These are decorated all over with green lacquer and gold chinoiseries in emulation of the fantasies of Chinese decoration. This English furniture owes its shapes entirely to Dutch forms but a large part of its glory lies in

15
*A rare pair of
Charles II brass
andirons with
enamel decoration.*

16
*An Anglo-Indian
ebony centre table,
inlaid with ivory in
the Moghul style.
Circa 1680.*

17
*A green lacquer
dressing table of
about 1690,
still with its toilet
mirror en suite.*

the exotic oriental taste of its decoration. The toilet mirror has its original mirror plate, bevelled around the edges and with a central star cut in it. Dressing tables such as this were sometimes flanked by a matching pair of candle stands or torchères. We recently had a pair of such stands, with a table, that are also representative of the close links between Holland and England at the end of the seventeenth century (fig. 18). The turned stems of these stands have a beautiful simplicity and rhythm; their overall proportions are perfect. In addition, the contrasting colours and character of the chosen kingwood veneers add greatly to their timeless charm. The turned stems are of solid kingwood.

A very rare and beautiful object is a William and Mary centre table

18

In the Dutch manner, this pair of candle stands, or torchères, are entirely of solid and veneered kingwood. Circa 1690.

19

A William and Mary centre table of scagliola, imitating pietra dura, *the top with a vase and cornucopia of flowers.*

29

21

A rare Louis XIV bureau mazarin decorated with imitation Chinese coromandel incised and polychrome lacquer.

(fig. 19) from Warwick Castle and acquired by the Victoria and Albert Museum in 1968. 3 ft 10 in. wide, the top, and also the frieze are decorated in scagliola with a vase and cornucopia of flowers, and groups of birds and flowers. The legs are also of simulated marble and the stretcher is similarly decorated.

20

A very rare late seventeenth century kingwood cabinet mounted with superb Florentine pietra dura *panels, on a walnut and kingwood stand of later date, with magnificent carved cabriole legs.*

French furniture with decoration in the Chinese manner is represented by a very rare Louis XIV bureau mazarin with panels simulating coromandel lacquer incised and painted in polychrome (fig. 21) The top has characteristic Chinese rock forms amidst flowers that betray a European hand. The writing table has a long drawer running the full width of the piece and shorter ones below. The lacquer may perhaps have been done by Gérard Dagly, or even his brother Jacques who settled in Paris.

A magnificent late seventeenth century cabinet which Mallett sold in 1947 has once again returned to Bond Street (fig. 20). This is of kingwood and walnut and is in two parts, a cabinet upon a stand. The cabinet itself might be Dutch or English; it is beautifully constructed with walnut lined drawers and faced with cross-bandings of kingwood. Its chief purpose is to display a superb collection of mid-seventeenth century Florentine *pietra dura* panels, inlaid marble pictures of birds, flowers and fruit together with smaller pieces of naturally figured Tuscan *albarese* marble, also known as *pietra paesina*. Brass key plates and knobs for the individual drawers add a further richness. The cabinet stands on a base of walnut, with a kingwood moulding and with larger drawers, and stands on splendidly carved legs, typical of the first quarter of the eighteenth century. The piece thus incorporates earlier treasured marbles in a cabinet upon a later stand created to support it, the whole a masterpiece of trans-European collecting and cabinet making.

With this Anglo-Dutch and Florentine transitional cabinet we see English furniture confidently established as having its own very special character, one of simple elegance enriched from time with well mannered ornament and always proud of judicious use of fine woods. Those were to be the continuing strengths and virtues of English taste through the eighteenth century.

22
A rare early seventeenth century Indian cabinet of European form with Moghul ivory inlay including Chinese cloud motifs. This precious chest for treasures represents a worldwide fascination in magnificent cabinets for combined storage and display.

23
A Chinese export coromandel lacquer cabinet of about 1700 is decorated with dramatic landscapes populated with horsemen and courtiers.

24
A large panel of Chinese incised coromandel lacquer shows mythological birds and flowers on one side, the reverse having figures in a courtly setting.

33

If furniture could talk

———⟨⟨⟨◇⟩⟩⟩———

WHEN I completed *Great English Furniture* in 1991, I quickly realised that a far more entertaining book than a history of the subject would have been stories about each piece's fate and relationship with its various owners. The furniture's view of its owners might have been revealing.

My colleagues and I can certainly recall numerous amusing incidents of discovery, acquisition and ownership. In a place where there is so much that is beautiful and many of the finer items are worth at least as much as an expensive house, it is understandable that furniture can inspire avaricious passion and heart rending 'love affairs' can be acted out dramatically on occasion. But reason also triumphs. An old friend of Mallett once visited the shop with her small daughter. When she found an elegant cabinet that she had a perfect use for, and which she liked very much, the down-to-earth child pointed out that its cost was the equivalent to that of several workmen's cottages. The mother's dream was shattered. But I shall refer to several more successful furniture romances during the course of this book.

The splendid pieces we handle are an international commodity and some have travelled widely. How astonished would the cabinetmakers be, who made them in the small streets of London. It is not unusual for a particular item to have crossed the Atlantic several times and it is not considered remarkable that quite large pieces are sent hither and thither across continents and oceans to be shown in exhibitions and trade fairs. The great *Treasure Houses of Britain* exhibition held in Washington in 1985, amassed an astonishing quantity of large and valuable heritage objects.

Speaking of travelling reminds me of a piece of furniture with a homing instinct. We were approached by an owner regarding a magnificent table that he wished to dispose of. Would we come and view it in an apartment on Fifth Avenue in New York? Certainly. Next time we were there it was seen and was purchased for the business. It was brought back to London by expert carriers as usual, beautifully packed, crated, insured, shipped,

25
A very fine eighteenth century bureau bookcase, with broken pediment, of walnut richly veneered with tortoiseshell and inlaid with ivory details, possibly Antwerp, circa 1735. It is flanked by a pair of Queen Anne japanned hall chairs and rococo wall lights.

un-crated, unpacked, polished up a little and put on display in Bond Street. Two weeks later or so it was purchased by an American once more, packed, shipped and so forth, to another apartment in the very same building on Fifth Avenue.

That tale of course seems laughable, and illustrates a strange coincidence. But more importantly it reflects the fact that London does still remain at the centre of much of the art market and provides the main part of the expertise in English Furniture. The trouble and cost of taking objects back and forth overseas is secondary to the efficient and practical business of acquiring and marketing valuable top quality articles. Naturally we feel sorry for the poor old pieces sometimes but they are greatly treasured thoroughbreds and every possible cosseting is given to them in transit.

Mallett's have now held four triennial exhibitions in Australia, taking a broad range of furniture, pictures, objects and textiles to Martyn Cook's premises in Sydney. On these occasions we have sent many millions of pounds worth, without problems. Transportation is an expensive operation but is competitive not only in terms of price but also in efficiency. Hardly any damage has occurred over the years and certainly nothing more serious than the coming apart of a glued joint. We had a near miss on the last occasion however. A set of four magnificent porcelain fruit coolers from a large dinner service 'went missing' escaping the hawkeyes and gentle attention of the two men who travelled with the consignment. They turned up later, beautifully packed in the locked drawers of a cabinet.

Unusual occurrences are amongst the most memorable. They are not typical of our normal calm business in helping clients select and purchase an appropriate piece. Very often this is a long process carefully considered by both sides. Occasionally however there is an instant 'love affair' and an immediate decision and that needless to say causes a thrill for both client and salesman, each trying to keep their cool. A customer who I knew well came into the shop on a particular occasion at least twenty years ago. As we reached the furthest room on the lower level she stopped in the doorway, spotted a Carlton House desk in the middle of the room, pointed and said to me rather definitely, 'I'll take that one please', upon which she turned around and walked back. There were others in the room, but on first glance she knew that that was exactly what she had always wanted, recognised it instantly as very special, and was going to take no risks in delaying.

It was in that same last room that I had another, less satisfactory experience, with a grand lady whose habit was to walk through viewing objects and to instruct me on the return journey of a list of pieces she wished to purchase. We had not seen her for some years but eventually she appeared and we set forth on our usual routine and discussed all sorts of interesting and lovely objects. As we reached that famous last room and were about to turn back her hand felt around her neck and she exclaimed 'My God, the jewels, I left them in the hotel' upon which she rushed out of the shop and we didn't see her again for a long time. When she comes in nowadays I always notice her jewellery.

The search and demand for fine antiques will I am sure carry on for ever but the uses for them will vary. In overhearing a conversation recently about the arrangement of certain rooms it gradually became apparent that this was for an aeroplane! Fine things can surely come into a new life on planes or yachts – they are ever adaptable to human circumstances.

26
A pair of Japanese lacquer brûle parfum urns, with aventurine decoration and gold flowers, with ormolu mounts, circa 1800. Reputedly the property of Empress Josephine.

27
This elegant George III sideboard is decorated with neo-classical inlay in satinwood on the gently curving drawer fronts. The cache pots are Paris porcelain and the glass bowl is Irish.

37

Walnut –
Early Eighteenth Century

⬦⬦⬦⬦⬦⬦⬦⬦⬦⬦⬦

AT the beginning of the eighteenth century, walnut was the most highly prized wood for making fine furniture. The excellent colour of this material, combined with the elegant proportions and simple lines favoured at this time, made this one of the most wonderful periods of English furniture making. This was the basis for the Georgian period which triumphed in wave after wave of fine pieces in ever evolving styles.

The first decade or so of the century is often known as the Queen Anne period; the monarch reigned from 1702 to 1714. That term cannot be used too strictly since characteristics varied and survived with little consistency in different regions.

A writing desk or bureau (fig. 31) is emblematic of the simple and elegant furniture of the first decade of the eighteenth century. Above all it has superb colour in the veneers and mouldings which have gained excellent varied tones in the patination over nearly three hundred years. The turned bun feet and the cock-bead mouldings framing the drawer fronts are an interesting hang-over from furniture of the previous reign, that of William and Mary. A writing or games table (fig. 32) also has earlier features, having straight turned legs, an angular top with wide overhang and, again, small bun feet. At the back two legs swing out in gate fashion to support the folding top. Also with a fold-over top, but this time hinging forwards onto sliding lopers is a bachelor's chest (fig. 29) which is said to have been so called on account of its all purpose use while dressing, powdering a wig, writing and reading. The walnut used for the veneers on this magnificent piece is carefully selected for its figuring and successive pages (i.e. slices with similar grain character) are used in balanced reflecting formation, a feature that was continuously practised in all woods throughout the century, and especially on drawer fronts.

Tables of many useful forms were made in delightful proportions and with the choicest walnut. A writing and reading table (fig. 30) of the same period, that is of about the first decade of the eighteenth century, has solid

28

The Rodney cabinet, a superb early eighteenth century walnut bureau bookcase with the unusual feature of folding doors enclosing the writing section. The top doors are fronted with mirrors, as are the small interior doors. (See pages 48 and 50.)

29
A handsome walnut bachelor's chest of about 1710 with a top which folds forward on to slides.

30
A charming and superbly made walnut library table with an adjustable book support. Circa 1710.

31
This walnut veneered Queen Anne bureau is distinguished by fine proportions and superb colour.

32
A walnut table with a folding top and gate-leg supports at the back. Circa 1700.

33
Queen Anne walnut furniture has no cluttering ornament, just fine proportions and elegant lines.

34
Brass handles and key escutcheons are usually the only ornamental features on early walnut furniture. A side table of circa 1710.

35

An early eighteenth century walnut kneehole desk, the top fitted with a mirror and compartments.

walnut legs but the tip-up top and concave sides are of strongly marked burr walnut. The top has re-entrant corners and two candle slides are fitted at the sides. This and another charming small sized table (fig. 33), have plain pad feet typical of their time and each has a drawer in the frieze, concealed in the second, and operated from the underside.

A side table (fig. 34) shows progressively more curvaceous 'cabriole' legs in comparison with the two tables shown previously and has an elegantly shaped frieze. The smart brass handles and key escutcheon on the drawers add ornament.

Another popular furniture form of this earlier walnut period was the kneehole desk, a small chest of drawers with a recessed central cupboard, sometimes with a discreet (non-handled) drawer at the top of the kneehole, as in the case of fig. 35. An unusual feature of this one is the lift-up top containing a mirror and numerous small compartments for dressing and writing.

36
*A small
Queen Anne
walnut bureau
standing on
cabriole legs,
of wonderful colour.*

An alternative form for similar uses, is seen in fig. 36, a charming small bureau on stand with elegant solid walnut legs. The ring handles are an earlier type than the larger drop handles on the two pieces described previously but there was a considerable overlap in types used. An even more precious miniature bureau cabinet is shown in fig. 37. This rare form must have been very expensive for it has a mirror panel in the door of the upper section and a candle could be placed on a slide fitted above the writing flap. There is also an additional folding slide above the four lower drawers.

37
A miniature walnut bureau cabinet of about 1710, the upper part enclosed behind a precious mirror plate.

Greatly in contrast in scale is a bookcase of unusually large proportions (fig. 40). Derived in form from oak bookcases of a type associated with Samuel Pepys, this has a low waist, with just two drawers in the base and a maximum amount of shelving contained behind large glass panes, still an expensive material in the early eighteenth century.

The use of solid carved walnut is admirably featured in two stools. The earlier one (fig. 38) has the familiar pad feet, but the legs are supported by very unusual and elegant flying brackets. The second stool (fig. 39) has a drop-in seat and is of about a decade later, perhaps circa 1720, with

38

*A fine Queen Anne
walnut stool with
'flying buttress'
corner brackets.*

39

*Another very good
early eighteenth
century walnut stool
with ball and claw
feet and with very
fine needlework.
Circa 1720.*

characteristic carved legs, having ball and claw feet (ultimately of ancient Chinese origin) and with classical acanthus leaf carving at the knees. The nature of the wood has once again contributed here to a superb nuttiness of colour. The needlework in both cases is also magnificent. On the second stool is a previously unused panel of the period which we found fitted the stool perfectly. The design with a basket of flowers and with sheep below is especially charming.

Folding tables were extremely useful in the relatively small rooms of Queen Anne period houses for they could be kept against the wall and would be brought out for different uses especially for eating and for playing games. Several walnut card tables must be shown. An exceptionally elegant pair of small half-round tables (fig. 41), stand on simple cabriole legs with pad feet. Finely veneered and crossbanded with burr walnut they have fold-back tops that rest on single gate legs. Small drawers in the frieze were no doubt a useful place for storing playing cards or games pieces.

Three further folding card tables have in common cabriole legs terminating in claw and ball feet and each opens on to a pair of sliding back legs fitted in concertina fashion. The first (fig. 42) is the more curvilinear, displaying earlier Dutch influence with a shaped frieze and with especially interesting carving at the knee and elegantly inward turning scrolls. The rounded corners provide platforms for candlesticks when the table is open. The next table (fig. 43) shows this feature together with indented wells for games counters or money. This table has a gadrooned moulding along the front and on the knees. A popular motif on early Georgian furniture is a scallop shell, here with a pendant leaf motif and below a carved moulding which cleverly conceals the join where the veneered side of the table meets the solid leg. The third of these card tables (fig. 44) looks forward to the period of mahogany with a more rectangular top, squared off corners and with most elegant legs finely carved with bold scrolls and extremely elongated acanthus leaves. Once again the nut-brown patination and colour is outstanding. The carved aspects of each of these games tables would

40

*A fine early
eighteenth century
walnut bookcase
with glass doors, in
two sections, the
lower part with
drawers.*

41

A beautiful pair of small sized walnut card tables suited to the relatively small rooms of Queen Anne houses.

suggest that they date from the second decade of the eighteenth century and are therefore often termed George I, who reigned from 1714 to 1727.

The most extravagant form of furniture made at this time was the bureau bookcase, at full size a large standing cabinet with a desk and drawers at the base and surmounted by a cabinet of plain shelves or even fitted with numerous compartments and drawers, enclosed behind a pair of mirror fronted doors. Two outstanding examples must be illustrated here, both of about 1720. Firstly, fig. 46 shows a classic and beautiful example of its kind. The fall front bureau opens to reveal compartments and small drawers. The upper section has mirror plates supported on the outer sides by elegant tapering pilasters with gilded capitals. The broken arch pediment encloses a carved and gilded figure of Atlas. This splendid cabinet formerly belonged to Benjamin Wyatt, father of the famous eighteenth century architect James Wyatt, as testified by an old letter that is preserved in a drawer.

The second bureau bookcase (figs 45 and 28, shown on page 38) is of an extremely unusual form having, instead of a fallfront writing flap, a pair of sloping foldback doors which reveal the traditional writing compartment together with a pull out writing slide. The drawer fronts on the outside are edged with brass moulding and the piece has relatively ornate engraved brass handles and key escutcheons with folding cover plates. There are ornamental carrying handles on the sides of the upper and lower halves of the cabinet. The top, again with a broken pediment supports three carved

42

43

44
Three very fine walnut card tables dating to the reign of George I, with differing shapes and ornament but all with carved claw and ball feet.

45
The Rodney cabinet, a superb early eighteenth century walnut bureau bookcase with the unusual feature of folding doors enclosing the writing section. The interior is fitted with numerous drawers, compartments and secret places behind columns. (See also fig. 28, page 38.)

46

This fine early eighteenth century walnut bureau bookcase belonged to Benjamin Wyatt. It has mirror plate doors flanked by slender pilasters and a carved giltwood figure of Atlas in the pediment.

giltwood figures of classical form. The interior of the piece is richly fitted with small drawers, pairs of mirrored doors enclosing cupboards and further carved figures standing on columns which pull forward to reveal secret compartments. This remarkable piece of furniture once belonged to Lord Rodney, a famous eighteenth century naval commander and it has since been known as the Rodney cabinet. (I wrongly attributed this name to a somewhat similar bureau bookcase in my book of 1991.) Certain elements in the form of this piece could perhaps mean that it was made in Germany rather than England; many qualities and features were shared at the time.

47
This pair of Queen Anne walnut side chairs retains its original red needlework with a water lily design.

48
Elegant George I side chairs such as these were sometimes made in extensive sets and were placed against the walls of a room, to be drawn up when required.

49

*One of an elegant
pair of early
eighteenth century
walnut side chairs
with parcel gilt
carving and
mouldings.*

From cabinets I now wish to turn to seat furniture of the first third of the eighteenth century. The making of chairs was a very different craft requiring quite separate skills. While an expert use of veneers was not as prominent, carving could be much richer but above all was the importance of achieving a strong weight-bearing form that still had an elegant sculptural appearance. The development of these chairs form the box-like stools of mediaeval times had reached extraordinary heights that continued to be increasingly elegant throughout the century.

The fine upholstered side chairs (side chairs are without arms) of fig. 47 are of the Queen Anne period, of about 1710. Designed to be comfortable and rich looking they are upholstered with the original magnificent needlework with a most unusual pattern of large water-lily flowers and leaves shown on a red background. The elegant cabriole front legs are enhanced with long C-scrolls at the knees while the back legs are also nicely curved. In inferior chairs less trouble was taken in making the back legs which didn't show much, as all chairs were placed against the walls of a room. For this same reason no chairs are decorated on their

50

A fine pair of George I side chairs enriched with carved detailing, and with drop-in needlework seats.

backs, at any period, a convention that has lasted right up to modern times.

The next few illustrations show chairs and a settee with drop-in seats, that is, upholstered frames, often covered with needlework, that slip down into the seat of a chair frame.

Fig. 48 shows a pair of chairs of about 1720 with high shaped backs, with walnut back splats supported by curved uprights. The front surfaces of these are veneered with specially selected patterned walnut as are the outer faces of the deep seat frame. The long scrolls on either side of the back splats and the legs are of solid walnut finely shaped and carved.

Another chair of the earlier period, one of a pair (fig. 49) is unusual in having a finely shaped back with supports to the central splat forming interesting voids framed by the crossbanded uprights and cross bars. Each element is gently moulded at the edges and is gilded. This parcel gilding (partial gilding) is also applied to the carved scallop shell and acanthus ornament on the legs.

Looking at the open shapes on the backs of chairs and indeed the void framed by the overall leg structures gives one another approach to the elegance of many of the finer specimens. Fig. 50 shows another pair that display a magnificent use of walnut but this time enriched with carving in the backs, in the form of curled leaves edging a vase shape, and also mouldings, and with a delicate edging of gadroon moulding on the lower side of the seat frame. The chairs also retain very fine needlework seats.

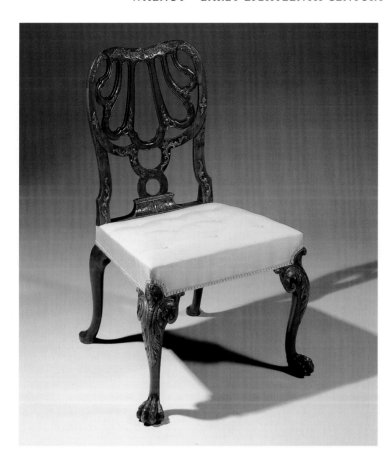

51

This walnut side chair is one of a well-known pattern attributed to Giles Grendey. The carving is partly gilded.

52

A double chair back settee with a drop-in seat covered in French needlework. The woods of the veneered back are contrasted with carving in the solid on the arms and legs. Circa 1720.

53

A wonderful pair of walnut side chairs. The strong, mannered design shows Dutch characteristics. English, circa 1720.

54

The early eighteenth century needlework seats of the walnut chairs shown in fig. 53 portray charming arcadian scenes within borders of garden flowers.

55

A walnut escutcheon-back library or cockfighting chair. Circa 1710.

The double chairback settee of fig. 52 was formerly in the Earl of Denbigh's house, Newnham Paddox. It has elegantly shaped and carved armrests and a particularly handsome back pattern with elaborate shapings and each splat centred with a panel of contrasting wood, perhaps holly. The needlework seat is French, as was used often on English furniture. Professionally made pieces were imported from Paris. In this case the fine needlework is not original to the sofa, though highly appropriate.

A magnificent pair of side chairs (figs 53 and 54) are elaborately curvi-linear, perhaps reminiscent of the Dutch influence that was behind so much English furniture of the time. Of about 1720, these chairs have almost exaggerated curves to the cabriole legs, a fine shell in half-relief on the fronts and lively contradicting curves to the back uprights, while the cresting of the backs is in a cartouche form and finely carved. The drop-in seats have very fine needlework of the period which we put on these chairs. Pictorial ovals framed by garden flowers show arcadian life, a maiden milking a red cow and another with her red spotted dog.

Still of walnut and having an elaborate shape is one of a number of chairs

56

Like the chair in fig. 55 this one has 'shepherds crook' arms. It is upholstered with fine contemporary needlework, possibly made for it in the early eighteenth century.

associated with the maker Giles Grendey (fig. 51). This chair has a back resembling a large shell of shaped mouldings enriched with carving, which is parcel gilt. The legs terminate in claw feet and have at the knees a form typical of Grendey, a curved tongue rising upwards while the knee itself is of scrolling acanthus leaf design.

Some interesting armchairs include two 'shepherds crook armchairs' named for the obvious reason that the armrest has a curious doubling back to the support. The first of these (fig. 55) has a curved escutcheon back, finely veneered, a generously wide seat and joining stretcher between the legs. This last feature is associated with earlier chairs, usually as a precursor of times when a chairmaker's supreme confidence in strength allowed him the added elegance of omitting it. In this case however the stretcher adds to the conceived weight of the design. The same is clearly part of the design of another charming chair of this kind (fig. 56) and in this case has a carved leaf at the otherwise weak crossing point of the stretchers. The delicate lines of the chair are enriched with fine needlework, with a parrot on the back and a swan on the seat.

57
This Queen Anne walnut sofa is still covered with its original very fine French St. Cyr needlework showing chinoiserie figures and 'bizarre' shapes against a blue silk ground.

Magnificent needlework coverings were a frequent feature of walnut seat furniture but only a very small amount has survived in good order, and in an unfaded state. This was often of fine amateur workmanship, especially in England but also sometimes professionally made and imported from France. A wonderful Queen Anne sofa of small scale but with a high back and with outward scrolling arms (fig. 57) is richly upholstered with finely worked needlework from the St Cyr factory in Paris, an organisation set up originally by Madame de Maintenon, after the death of Louis XIV. Point de St Cyr is characterised by a lively pattern incorporating chinoiserie figures and bizarre shapes adapted from Ottoman silks, seen sometimes against a blue silk ground as in this case. There is a set of side chairs in the Brooklyn Museum comparable to this sofa.

Much more representative however of England and an English garden is the floral needlework on another fine armchair of about 1720 (fig. 58). Here again, the arms have shepherds crooks while the legs have cartouches at the knees and ball and claw feet. The original needlework is rich and colourful with a brown ground.

58
The needlework on this early eighteenth century chair is wholly English in design, a massed collection of garden flowers.

59
*A magnificent
Queen Anne walnut
wing chair with its
original floral
needlework showing
exotic flowers and
leaves inspired by
Anglo-Indian
textiles.*

60
*A small walnut
centre table of about
1710, the top with
oyster-cut veneers
laid in concentric
circles.*

Especially remarkable is a wing chair or 'easy chair' as they were often
known, of about 1710 (fig. 59). This magnificent survivor has passed through
our galleries recently but also featured in our catalogue of 1936 where it was
illustrated and offered at £385. It was a good deal more expensive this time
but worth every penny! The generous and elegant shape is accentuated
by graceful legs and 'Spanish' toes but the quality and condition of the
needlework remains astonishing. The colourful exotic flowers and leaves,
derived from earlier English and Indian textiles, are shown against a very
finely worked mustard-brown ground.

Returning to some further unusual walnut pieces of the first part of the
eighteenth century I must single out two small tables. The first (fig. 60), of
about 1710, is a small centre table, finished on all sides and with a drawer in
one end. It has a remarkable top of oyster-cut veneers laid in concentric
circles with line decoration and stands on very elegant, slightly curved, legs.
The second table (fig. 61) is more elaborate with unusually rich carved

61

The carved apron of this early eighteenth century walnut table is unusually rich and the cabriole legs correspondingly elegant.

ornament on the shaped apron below the frieze, shell motifs on the knees and the more curvaceous legs end in Spanish toes. This side table was probably made in about 1720.

A magnificent walnut cabinet of the same date (fig. 63) consists of a cupboard with drawers below. Of richly figured burr walnut, the upper part has two doors with fielded panels framed with carved mouldings, and these are flanked by three fluted pilasters. At the base there is a richly carved plinth supported by short legs with claw feet. Another unusual item (fig. 62) is an early eighteenth century marriage of a Flemish strongbox made for the back of a carriage, placed on a stand, in the form of a cupboard. The good colour and elaborate brass mounts of the box are in delightful contrast.

As the eighteenth century proceeded there was a greater formality in design, more classicism in the drawing and this coincided with a change in fashion and the use of mahogany for fine furniture. In the meantime

62
*This period
'marriage' shows a
travelling chest and
writing cabinet
mounted on a
cabinet to form a
fixed piece of
furniture. The
colour of the walnut
is outstanding.
Circa 1710.*

63
A rare George I burr walnut linen or clothes cabinet, with pilasters on the upper part and an elegantly carved base.

64

Emblematic of the reign of George II is the grand architectural form of this parcel-gilt walnut mirror of about 1730.

furniture was sometimes seen of walnut conceived in the classical taste that followed influential designers such as William Kent. This was frequently partly gilded. Two examples are worth illustrating. Firstly, a mirror (fig. 64) with a tall vertical plate is framed within a grand architectural format of walnut enriched with giltwood carving. A broken swan-neck pediment at the top is centred by a splendid shell, and swags of flowers hang from

65

One of a magnificent pair of walnut side tables supporting black and gold marble tops and with gilt carving, made to a design by John Vardy, for the Duke of Bolton, circa 1761.

profile masks at the sides. The second example of the use of parcel gilt walnut is a magnificent pair of large side tables with black and gold marble tops, designed by John Vardy and made for the Duke of Bolton at Hackwood Park, Hampshire. One of the tables is shown in fig. 65. These represent an old fashioned use of walnut, having been made in about 1761. The friezes are carved with trelliswork and floral paterae and a large central cartouche displays the Duke's heraldic shield. The tables stand on bold cabriole legs with claw and ball feet and are grandly decorated with leaves, scrolls and chains, all highlighted with gold. Nothing could be much grander than these tables; they are the complete antithesis of the small-scale domestic tables and chests made for intimate Queen Anne rooms and described at the beginning of this chapter. With this palatial furniture of the mid eighteenth century we have arrived at a time when wealth and power were displayed as outwardly and opulently as possible. This can be compared with the richest French furniture, and yet for all their grandeur the English still built their greatest houses and decorated them in a noble yet relatively restrained manner that has helped to make this taste continuously and universally popular.

Lacquer

—⊰⊱⊰⊱⊱⊰⊰⊰⊰⊰⊙⊱⊱⊰⊰⊱⊰⊱—

CHINESE lacquer imported to Europe in the seventeenth century caused a sensation. Brought with porcelain, silks and spices from the East these 'Indian' wares were prized exotic luxuries that fascinated the rich. It was only vaguely known where the lacquer came from. Little distinction was made between India and China but the term Indian had some real significance in that most of the Chinese exports changed hands on the eastern coasts of India before being shipped from there to Europe. There was a complex chain of dealing and bartering where commodities were sent back and forth filling ships travelling in every direction. Much of the earliest lacquer brought to England came in the form of large folding screens, sizeable panels that were sometimes kept intact as screens but on other occasions were cut up to make wall panels, to make chests and to be used in smaller pieces on furniture. Tables, mirrors and cabinets would be made up from parts of screens, the exotic shapes and colours being used as we might now make a patchwork of precious fragments of textiles. A marriage chest (fig. 67) or trunk of circa 1700 is an example of the earlier form of Chinese export lacquer. Termed 'coromandel' probably because it was shipped via the Coromandel coast of East India, this form of lacquer is incised layers of resin decoration with colourful sculptured motifs, here executed in panels. While patterns were often on a large scale others, perhaps at the tops and bottoms of screens were in smaller sections. This chest is made up of a number of such panels, depicting typical semi-mythical animals, birds and flowers.

Coromandel lacquer was the earliest type used in English furniture and was followed by further gilded lacquer panels, mostly black though occasionally of other colours. This was flat, not incised, and richly decorated with Chinese landscapes, people, animals and buildings.

True oriental lacquer was the beginning of an even greater fashion, an art of creative imitation. The imitation was by no means a faithful copying but much more interestingly a Chinese inspired version of painting in the

A magnificent early eighteenth century English lacquer bureau bookcase decorated with gilt chinoiseries, a wholly European form with 'Chinese' decoration. The hoop-back chairs, of about 1770, are also japanned, in black with gold floral sprigs of flowers.

67
This chest of around 1700 is made up with panels of Chinese incised coromandel lacquer made for export.

oriental manner. Using various background colours as overall decoration, wonderful 'chinoiserie' forms were superimposed in gloriously fanciful, exotic and often slightly humorous forms in gold, and sometimes with other colouring. The effect was chiefly of gilded vignettes, birds, figures, animals, insects and flowers scattered carefully over a bright ground. Black was the first and most popular colour, inspired by the true Chinese lacquer but soon other brighter colours caught on: red, green, blue and even white. Red was perhaps the most beautiful, white is the rarest, and green, blue and blue-green can also be superb. This imitation lacquer was known as japanning, further showing geographical vagueness, and in part it was done by amateur women, decorating furniture supplied by a cabinetmaker. Much however was professionally made and we know of several suppliers.

A book of patterns by Messrs Stalker and Parker entitled *A Treatise on Japanning* published in 1668, shows some of the deliberately naïve motifs that were popularised. However many of the finer pieces of japanned furniture of the late seventeenth century, and especially of the early eighteenth century, display great quality in the painting and enormous charm. This decoration in conjunction with the fine proportions of Queen Anne furniture make this arguably the most glorious of all English furniture, and the perfect adjunct to other pieces of the period in walnut. Of course it has to be in good condition. It is not especially fragile but many pieces have been unnecessarily over-restored and once repainted they

68
Chinese lacquer cabinets of this form were exported to Europe and made into grand pieces of furniture with elaborate stands and crestings. This example demonstrates a further development in that the cabinet itself was made in England, in the Chinese fashion. Circa 1670.

invariably lose their charm. A magnificent scarlet japanned Queen Anne bureau bookcase is illustrated in fig. 66. This superb cabinet is of the traditional form with desk below and fitted shelves above, enclosed by expensive mirror doors. Here shown open, the piece is still bright red and decorated in a very un-Chinese manner with a great variety of gilt chinoiseries. An elegant double ogee pediment over the double domed

71

interior gives it tremendous stature, while the feet of 'bun' form, represent a hangover from the earlier William and Mary style. Marbleised columns flanking the two internal cupboards pull forward revealing secret compartments. The japanned chairs of loop form on either side of this piece are part of a set of about 1770, painted black and powdered all over with delicate flower sprigs in a chinoiserie manner. Unbelievably graceful, these epitomise the extraordinarily happy marriage of Eastern and Western cultural vision. The woodwork of the chairs is, incidentally, made up in laminated form, like plywood, in order to achieve sufficient strength.

Turning back to the middle of the seventeenth century we have a black lacquer cabinet on stand (fig. 68). This is representative of a great number of chests of this form that were imported to Europe from both Japan and China. Box-shaped they consist of a compact series of drawers enclosed by a pair of doors. The cabinets are decorated inside and outside (in the case of Japanese ones, sometimes on every side) with landscapes, figures, buildings and vases. The numerous hinges and the lock plates were usually of lightweight brass, pinned on, but soon these were replaced with heavier quality brasswork fitted with pins and screws when they arrived in Europe.

On arrival in England, such cabinets were transformed into a fine piece of furniture by being proudly mounted on a grand carved giltwood, or silvered base and sometimes also given magnificent crestings. This proud celebration of these oriental treasure chests reflects the fascination in such imported wonders. So prized were they that it soon became common to

70

A magnificent and rare William and Mary scarlet lacquer bachelor's chest with a folding top and many concealed drawers and compartments and wonderful chinoiserie decoration.

imitate the chests and many splendid chinoiserie cabinets were made, in various colours, and these were mounted on stands, as the original Chinese ones had been. The one illustrated here is indeed English being of good quality woodwork; and the japanning is also of great refinement. The stand and base are especially well carved in the Charles II manner and are silvered. This piece of furniture came from the Marquess of Bute's great house, Mount Stuart on the Isle of Bute, in the West Highlands of Scotland.

By the early eighteenth century English japanning and the imitation of Chinese cabinets had become very sophisticated. A fine example of Queen Anne period lacquer is a chest in white and red lacquer (fig. 69) with very pretty polychrome floral decoration, loosely based on oriental ideas though the layout of the design and the paintings is far from Chinese. Inside this

71

Japanning on a white ground was rare. Here a fine clock by Joseph Windmills has a case with a cream painted ground decorated with colourful chinoiserie motifs. Circa 1710.

piece there are numerous fitted drawers, also decorated with flowers, birds and animals on a white ground. A particularly remarkable piece of English furniture is an early eighteenth century red lacquer bachelor's chest (fig. 70). With several William and Mary features including bun feet, this rare piece has a fold-over top which rests on a pair of gate-legs that swing forward. Doors on either side of the front open to reveal pristine decoration on smaller drawers. The gold and black chinoiserie painting is very poetical. While walnut 'bachelor's chests', with fold-over tops, are seen relatively often, this is the only lacquered one that I have seen. The gate-leg form on a chest is also very rare; I know of one other, in walnut. It is however interesting to note the table in fig. 32, page 41. This red chest formerly belonged to Sir Philip Sassoon and was latterly at Houghton Hall, Norfolk where I remember being sent to see it soon after I joined Mallett's in 1969. It has now become part of another significant collection of furniture, in England.

I have mentioned that the rarest colour for japanned furniture is white (now toned inevitably to a warmer cream colour). A beautiful clock by

72

This late seventeenth century black japanned cabinet owes not only its decoration to Chinese origins. The upper part is derived from the shape of a chest, with added arcaded pediments. These retain their original carved giltwood crestings.

Joseph Windmills, circa 1710, is shown next (fig. 71). Windmills had become a Master of the Clockmakers' Company in 1702. The slender height of this timepiece (26 inches) makes it especially elegant. The cream lacquer is decorated with polychrome and gilt birds, flowers and pagodas. The dial is nicely inscribed 'Jos. Windmills, London' and the back plate is also finely engraved.

*The exterior of a
very fine Queen
Anne red lacquer
bureau bookcase
showing the aged
darker outside.*

Another black lacquer cabinet of William and Mary form (fig. 72) and
made in about 1690, has a double domed upper section standing on a chest
of drawers with arcaded feet. Richly ornamented with chinoiseries and
brasswork it also has fine carved giltwood crestings on each of the arched
pediments at the top, rare survivals of this kind of early baroque ornament.

Since one of the great high points of English furniture must be the superb
lacquer bureau bookcases of the early eighteenth century, and as these are a
great speciality for which Mallett's have been famed for generations, I shall
now look at some more pieces of this kind. Firstly, is a red lacquer cabinet
of circa 1710 (figs 73 and 74). In an excellent state of preservation and still
retaining a high proportion of untouched decoration with interesting
craquelure, this piece has a broken arched pediment above mirror doors

*74
The pristine scarlet
fitted interior of
the cabinet shown
in fig. 73.*

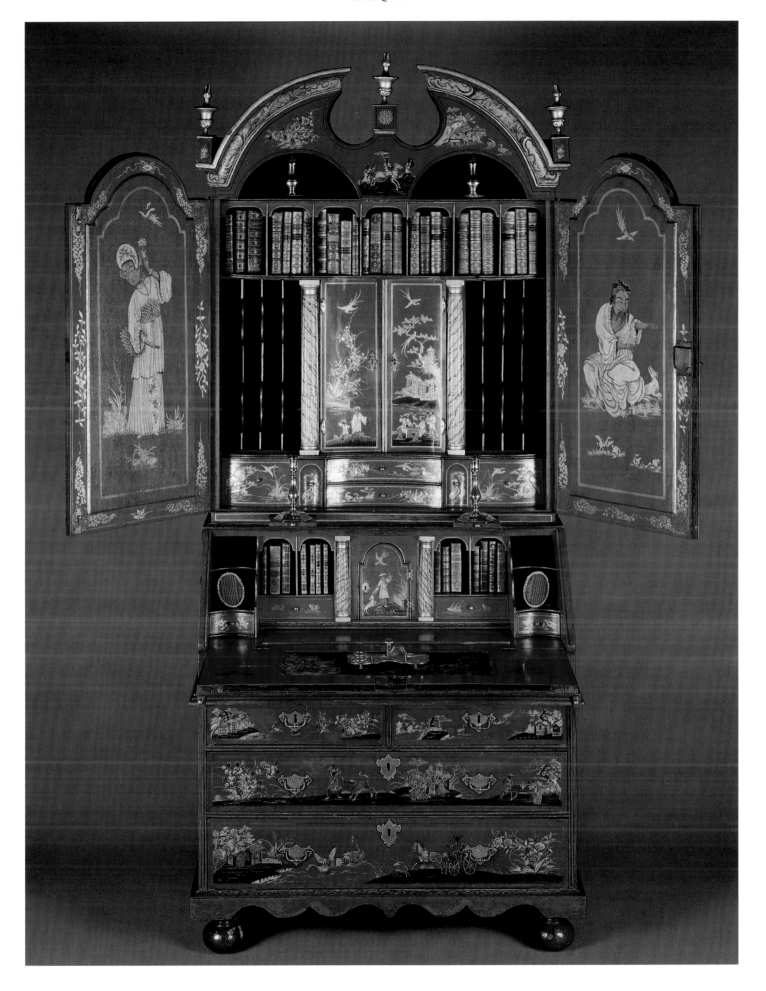

76
Occasionally lacquer bureau cabinets were made in pairs. These remarkable examples in red lacquer were united thirty years ago having been found in England and Spain. They found a new home in Portugal.

enclosing folio compartments, pigeonholes and marbled columns, which contain secret compartments. The colour of the outside has mellowed a little and the decoration has darkened with oxidisation while the interior remains very bright. Notice the elegantly shaped frieze at the base. A similar bureau cabinet, but this one with a double domed top is illustrated in fig. 276 on page 216 in a section about painted furniture. This piece has a scarlet interior with gold chinoiseries but, unusually, the exterior is of a different colour, black with colour added to the gilt decoration. Illustrated earlier, fig. 6, page 12, is an important and noble black japanned bureau bookcase of circa 1720 that compares in form with the walnut one shown on page 38. This remarkable cabinet is enormously tall, the bureau section being larger than usual. With a complex series of fittings the bureau itself is enclosed not by a fall-front slope but by double doors while a writing slide may be pulled forward. The upper part of the cabinet is elaborately fitted with small drawers, some in a smaller central compartment, enclosed by mirrored doors. A smaller black lacquer bureau bookcase with a single large mirror fronted door (fig. 75) has a bombé shaped base and a folding brushing slide above the three lowest drawers. In the top are pigeonhole compartments and shelves, lined in red. The chinoiserie decoration is made up entirely of garden landscapes.

75

A very charming small black lacquer bureau cabinet with a single mirror-fronted door.

78

Comparable in form to a walnut side table, this charming and rare Queen Anne example is entirely decorated with red japanning.

77

A very fine German green lacquer bureau bookcase of about 1730 with many shaped and carved features and richly decorated with gold chinoiseries.

A remarkable pair of small sized red lacquer cabinets (fig. 76) of similar form also have single mirror doors, bombé bases and brushing slides. They stand on shaped bracket feet and are decorated with individually different but similar chinoiseries. Mallett's acquired one of these in England and the other in Spain in 1969.

A further lacquer bureau bookcase, this time green, must be shown fig. 77). This interesting cabinet is German, rather than English, circa 1730. The concept of bureau cabinets such as all the ones I have discussed, originated in Holland in the second half of the seventeenth century. It was perfected in England and was subsequently adopted also in Germany and other European countries. German examples can be very rich in both construction and decoration, both in the case of wood veneered versions and lacquer ones. This soft lime-green piece is elaborately shaped with complex moulded drawers throughout, large and small, corinthian pilasters in the top section and a grand 'swan-neck' pediment at the top centred on a shell-framed and bearded mask. Though a later form of the 'Queen Anne' lacquer bookcase, marked most noticeably by the pediment, it retains the bun feet of twenty or thirty years earlier. The quality of the gold and variegated chinoiserie decoration is very fine and the piece is

also enhanced with elaborate ormolu handles on the main drawers.

Returning to England however we see in fig. 78 an unusual red japanned side table, circa 1710. With gently curved cabriole legs and a neat arrangement of long and short drawers this small table is richly ornamented with scenes, birds and flowers in gold chinoiseries, while drop handles with shaped brass back plates add another dimension of smartness.

Another large scale bracket or table clock (fig. 79) by George Clarke, Leadenhall Street, London has a fine japanned case with glass columns at the corners and cut glass and brass finials. The rich decoration is on a green

80

The delicacy of the floral painting on this cream lacquer toilet mirror of about 1710 resembles silk embroidery of the period.

ground. The clock has a musical movement with six tunes, the sound of which comes through the silk lined pierced fretwork above the dial and on the sides.

Another rare example of white (turned cream) lacquer is a Queen Anne toilet mirror (fig. 80) complete with its original bevelled mirror plate and with a shaped cresting above. Below is a small enclosed desk-like compartment fitted with small jewel drawers, and beneath this there is a larger drawer for powder boxes and brushes. The overall surface is sprinkled with flowers resembling embroidery on satin.

81

*A pair of European
pottery vases of
Japanese form are
decorated with rich
and mixed oriental
motifs.*

Also having a predominantly white ground is a pair of pottery vases
in the Japanese manner (fig. 81) probably of the eighteenth century.
Wondrously amorphic shapes with blue floral ornament creep across the
central reserve which is filled with 'chinoiserie' trees and birds. A pair of
Chinese dogs form finials in the traditional manner. Fig. 82 shows a
magnificent pair of scarlet lacquer side chairs of about 1725. These were
probably made for the Spanish or Portuguese market, possibly by Giles
Grendey of Clerkenwell who supplied furniture to the Duke of Infantado's
castle at Lazcano. The frames are somewhat solid with stretchers joining all
the legs but shapely nonetheless, with 'oriental' claw feet and crestings with
'Indian' busts and masks. The gilt chinoiseries show gardens, boats, small
boys, birds, flowers and fish. We also acquired a very similar pair of green
chairs from the same collection, clearly made in the same workshops.

Japanese lacquer is rather different to both Chinese and European
versions; for it is harder and glossier in both texture and line. It is extremely
crisp in execution. A fine trunk (fig. 84) of circa 1740 gives some idea of

82

*A very beautiful
pair of red lacquer
side chairs
attributed to
Giles Grendey who
supplied similar
furniture for export
to Spain.*

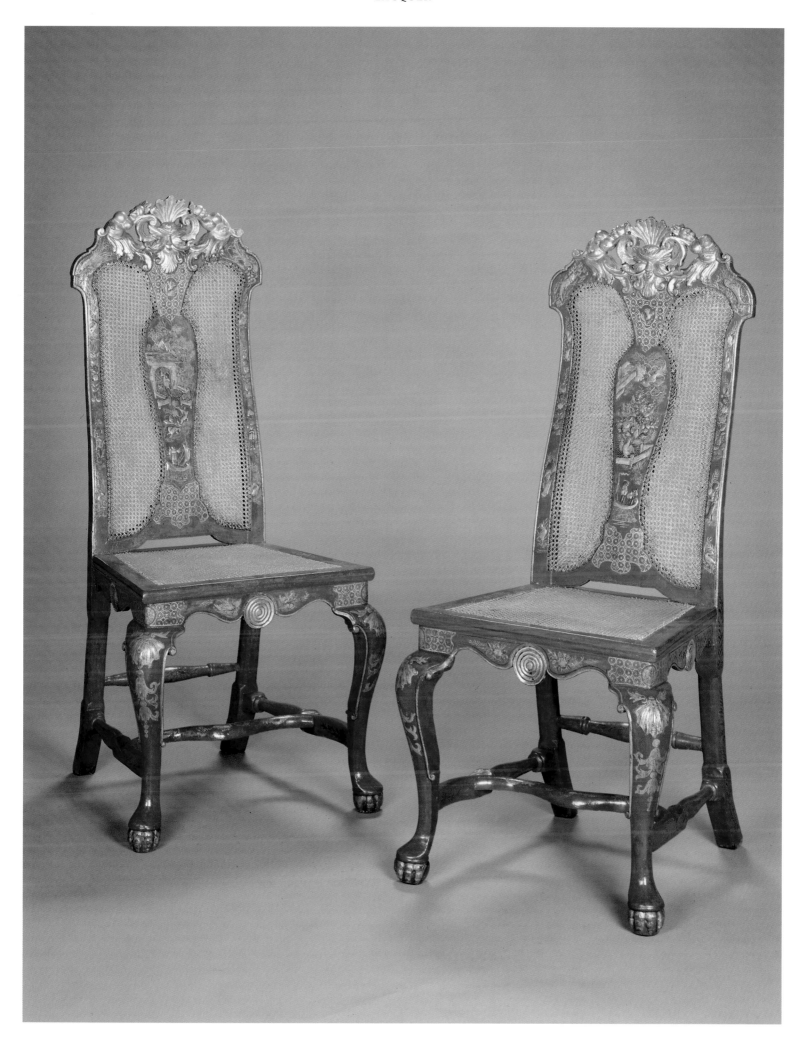

83
A pair of Berlin vases, circa 1725, decorated in red with raised Chinese motifs.

84
A Japanese lacquer trunk of the eighteenth century shows a more sharply defined variety of lacquer here with an overall design wound over the piece.

characteristic Japanese decoration. With a willow tree curled over it, the pictorial form is moulded over all the surfaces and the pattern is only broken by engraved gilt mounts. The lacquer decoration is built up in shaped relief. A pair of tall cylindrical vases (fig. 83) are of pottery overlaid with red lacquer and raised decoration. Attributed to Berlin, circa 1725, a similar technique was used also for other vases with lids, but these are especially large, being 34 inches high.

A charming English cabinet of about 1760 (fig. 85) in the Chippendale manner incorporates some treasured true Chinese lacquer on the top and veneered on the central concave doors. The other elements were made around these and decorated with delicate chinoiseries in keeping. The pierced fret gallery in a key-like pattern and trellage panels in the front continue the pseudo-Chinese theme in playful homage to wonders of the East.

It seems that almost anything could be decorated in the Chinese manner from furniture to the smallest household objects including porcelain and relatively ordinary crockery. Musical instruments were no exception. A

beautiful French harp of circa 1775 (fig. 86) shows neo-classical elements happily wedded with Chinese type painting with Chinese musicians and other figures in colours as well as gold, on a black ground. This Louis XVI instrument is by Godefroi Holtzmann of Paris and is exactly of the type that Mozart would have been familiar with.

I mentioned at the beginning of this section that Chinese lacquer was first imported to Europe in the form of screens and chests. I shall now mention two later screens. The first is of leather, perhaps Spanish (fig. 87), circa 1750, in six folds and decorated on a grey-blue ground with palace buildings, numerous figures, vases of flowers and birds. Screens such as this were light to move, very colourful and most useful for draught protection or privacy. On other occasions rooms might be entirely lined with decorated leather, using it like wallpaper, which was also popular, but in that case, almost invariably Chinese made.

The second screen (fig. 90) is a very richly decorated Chinese export one

87

A mid-eighteenth century leather screen painted with oriental buildings, people and flowers vaguely in the manner of Chinese screens.

86

Any object, even a magnificent Louis XVI harp, might be decorated with chinoiseries in approximate imitation of oriental lacquer.

of black and gold lacquer, circa 1820, probably from Canton. One side depicts a continuous scene of court life with courtiers and attendants amidst pavilions and pagodas in a landscape of rocks, trees and waterways with sampans, and rice farming. The other side (illustrated) is also richly decorated with a great lake view and further views with figures engaged in rural and domestic pursuits, all within a border of fierce entwined dragons and cloud formations.

A very special documented example of English furniture designed to incorporate Chinese export lacquer is the secretaire cabinet supplied by Thomas Chippendale for Harewood House in 1773. Shown in fig. 88, this remarkable piece was jointly acquired by Hotspur, Partridge Fine Arts and Mallett and subsequently bought for Temple Newsam House, Leeds, in memory of Christopher Gilbert, the furniture historian and former director of the museum. Faced with large panels of black and gold Chinese lacquer, this secretaire cabinet in neo-classical form is closely associated with other pieces made for Harewood House, especially a great commode which Mallett's handled twenty-five years ago. The commode was shown in *Mallett's Great English Furniture*, the forerunner to this volume, and is now in Jon Gerstenfeld's collection. The writing cabinet, made for the state bedchamber, was invoiced to Edwin Lascelles on 12th November 1773 by Thomas Chippendale as follows:

> 'A Lady's Secretary veneer'd with your own Japan with additions of Carved Ornaments &c japann'd and part Gilt, the front of the Secretary to rise with Balance Weights £26.0.0'.

Of neo-classical form, in the French manner of a secretaire abattant, this piece is very similar to another acquired by the National Trust for Osterley Park which had been recorded in that house in 1782. This was also supplied by Chippendale, probably using more of the Chinese lacquer provided by Edwin Lascelles. The Harewood secretary (fig. 88), it would seem, was just part of a sizeable commission which according to the 1795 inventory consisted of a 'State Bed with Dome Top in Burnished Gold Y one Japan Commode Y two India Cabinets Y One India Box Y One India Chimney Glass.' The fact that it is not itself mentioned in this list, it is suggested, was probably because it had been moved to the Lascelles' London house in Hanover Square. While most of the lacquer is true Chinese, including small drawer fronts fitted in the interior, there are a few additions of japanning to make up certain areas.

In some ways this fascinating 'secretary' brings us full circle in an extraordinary combination of cultures, influences and styles. It is obviously an important piece of furniture designed and provided by England's most famous cabinetmaker and designer for a patron whose country house was to become a temple of design and an influential example in terms of the decorative arts. But in addition the piece owes much to 'international' taste. Firstly, the cabinet is of a French form, never widely popular in Britain, but here provided as an exciting, useful and fashionable novelty, an experiment that was subsequently considered so successful that a second very similar version was made for Mr Childe's Osterley Park. Secondly, in terms of lacquer this substantial, rather than simply decorative item, represents some of the best mid-eighteenth century furniture where true Chinese lacquer of the export type (in panel form, not fully constructed furniture) is seen to

88

This 'Lady's Secretary' is a rare documented example of furniture supplied by Thomas Chippendale and especially interesting in that it incorporates Chinese export lacquer.

89
A Chinese export lacquer chest of drawers, circa 1770, is richly decorated with auspicious symbols, flowers and butterflies on a geometric ground. The drawers are fitted with a mirror and compartments for porcelain wash bowls.

eclipse the earlier eighteenth century preference for European lacquer. In the seventeenth century, as I have shown, Chinese export lacquer became highly fashionable and prized, both in cut-up form and as entire Chinese culture 'curios' (see figs 23, 24 and 67 for example). But through the first half of the eighteenth century it was japanning that was used on the most coveted and elegant furniture, as we have seen throughout this chapter. The great lacquer bureau bookcases and many cabinets of Chinese appearance were beautifully decorated with chinoiseries on a variety of coloured grounds. By the Chippendale period this seems to have waned in desirability and there was a return to the practice of making furniture incorporating panels of real Chinese lacquer, almost invariably black and showing Chinese landscapes in gold. The furniture making was by this time highly sophisticated and the same process and combination was also practised in France.

But England went further than France in another aspect and this grew into a further new and fascinating genre. We developed a taste and market for a fresh dimension in true export lacquer, wholly made pieces of furniture constructed and decorated in China in a new 'pretty' manner. More is said of Chinese exports in another chapter, including lacquer furniture. Here however, I shall show just one interesting piece that may be considered alongside Lady Lascelles' secretary. This is the Chinese lacquer chest of drawers shown in fig. 89, constructed and made in China for export to England, and designed to a classic eighteenth century English format typical of the 'Chippendale' period. The decoration is delightful but the motifs are very different; while the secretaire lacquer has traditional landscapes, the chest is ornamented with auspicious symbols and flowers on an overall geometric background. The woodwork is lightly, and by English standards, crudely constructed, mimicking an English form. The lacquer decoration is very different in spirit to the landscape 'screen' panels as on the Harewood cabinet. This decorative Chinese answer to the European chinoiseries that had been the rage for so long represents a new phase in both oriental lacquer and country house taste. It too was to enjoy phenomenal success. The drawers of this chest are fitted with compartments. The top one contains a dressing slide and fold-up mirror and small compartments while the second and third form a single deep drawer with further compartments for porcelain wash bowls, no doubt also provided by the Chinese.

The screen (fig. 90), already referred to, shows a later and further development in Chinese lacquer, with even more complex scenery incorporating endless vignettes. With such a colossal wealth of countryside, life and creativity, is it any wonder that we in the West have been so fascinated by Chinese decorative art and ornament?

90
This Chinese export lacquer screen of about 1820 is covered on both sides with a colossal wealth of life and activity in landscape settings, beautifully painted.

Mahogany –
The Mid Eighteenth Century

MAHOGANY is probably the most familiar wood of antique furniture. It is therefore difficult to understand now how special and how highly valued this material was in the eighteenth century. It was like gold. It was a new substance brought from far away at considerable risk, in limited quantities and was very costly. Only the rich could aspire to ordering things made of it.

The bureau bookcase shown opposite (fig. 91 and also frontispiece) was extremely expensive when it was made in about 1760 and it is the finest mahogany cabinet that Mallett have been lucky enough to handle in the last few decades. Its proportions are perfect, divided between writing section, drawers below, bookcase above and crowned with a glorious broken pediment with a central urn upon a pedestal. The cabinet represents the best of mid-eighteenth century furniture in general and especially Chippendale furniture, a classification that embraces everything made in the forms and styles associated with him. The quality of the mahogany chosen is the best, having a rich colour and fine figuring for the veneered parts and it lends itself to very crisp carving of details as in the mouldings, especially in the cresting. The close grain and strength of the wood allowed for the finely made astragals in the two glazed doors that enclose the bookshelves. The illustration at the opening of this book shows the bureau closed and we can see the veneering on the slope front and the bas-relief carving that frames it. Finely made rococo brass handles gently ornament the drawer fronts, without excess.

Mahogany is a close-grained, hard wood that was especially favoured by the English for fine furniture making, only becoming popular and widely used in France in the late eighteenth century and with the Empire style. First recognised by the carpenter on Sir Walter Raleigh's ship, in 1595 it was not until the earlier part of the eighteenth century that it became imported in significant quantity to Britain from Central America and the West Indies, particularly Jamaica. At this point it quickly became fashionable, its

91

An exceptionally fine mahogany bureau bookcase of the Chippendale period, the fall-front of the bureau section opens to reveal a leather writing surface and numerous small drawers and compartments. English, circa 1760.

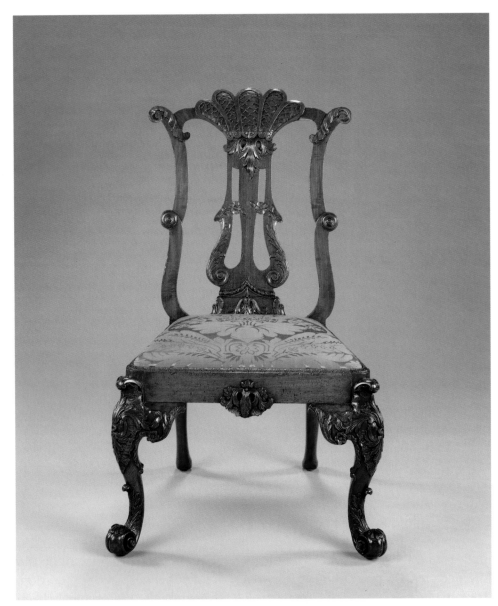

92

One of six mahogany chairs almost certainly made by Giles Grendey, the veneered surfaces of the backs contrasted with rich carving, including a fish-scale fan or shell motif at the top. Circa 1745.

qualities of fine colouring, grain texture and suitability for carving being recognised.

Of all the eighteenth century furniture designers Thomas Chippendale is the most famous and his name is especially associated with mahogany though his family business produced much marquetry furniture, painted furniture and other items in addition. Chippendale's name is associated mainly with the rococo style rather than to other pieces known to have been supplied by him or his son, due to his publication of a very influential book of patterns, *The Gentleman and cabinet maker's director* in 1754. This volume, as with so many pattern books, is truly a synthesis of fashionable styles of the period, many already devised by contemporaries, but there is no doubt that Thomas Chippendale was a prominent supplier of ideas as well.

Less familiar names are also celebrated as influential suppliers of furniture in the middle of the eighteenth century and these are becoming better known. I have already mentioned Giles Grendey when discussing both walnut and lacquer furniture. We recently sold six magnificent chairs

These are part of a remarkable set of sixteen, including a pair of armchairs, attributed to William Hallett, circa 1750.

attributed to this maker (fig. 92). These well-known chairs are wonderfully shapely with design elements related to several similar but variant patterns. They have drop-in seats supported on boldly sculptural legs, richly carved and ending in scrolling toes. The splendid lyre-shaped backs can clearly be seen as transitional between walnut splat back chairs and the rococo forms familiar to the Chippendale period but with a somewhat William Kent leaning towards the classical grotto taste for architectural scrolling and fish-scaled ornament. Here the tops of the backs have a fan or shell shaped cresting with fish-scale carving.

Amongst interesting chair designers were Matthew Darly and William Hallett whose interesting chair patterns include original forms with loop shaped backs. By extraordinary chance we have had two great sets of chairs made to a design with this feature of about 1750. These were a set of fourteen and a set of sixteen, both remarkable for their number. The difference between the two variants was in the feet only, in one case they had pad feet with leaf carving and in the other strong scroll toes. Fig. 93

shows two of the latter set. The hooped backs are faced with fine cross-banded veneering while the legs are carved with an intertwined ribbon pattern. The similar chairs have an interesting background in that they were supplied to Sir James Dashwood for the dining room at Kirklington Park, Oxfordshire between 1747 and 1752. The room itself with fine plasterwork was removed from the house many years ago and is now installed in the Metropolitan Museum, New York. The larger set is also shown in fig. 3 on page 8.

With most furniture, even of very high quality it is not possible to establish who designed or made it. There were a number of excellent small workshops and in England signatures were never attached to even the finest pieces. That was not considered necessary, or of interest. A beautiful Irish side table of about 1750 for example (fig. 94), is a piece that would have been made for a specific client and place. The journeyman and cabinetmaker would have used elements of design that were selected from a grammar of ornament that must have been of second nature to him, possibly to support a specific marble slab. This one is probably not the original.

English fashion and taste have always kept an eye on France and often borrowed ideas from across the channel. Fig. 95 shows one of a pair of mid-eighteenth century mahogany chairs that clearly have the reasonably stiff but still curvilinear lines of rococo scrolling. It is difficult to say whether these reflect Régence pre-rococo formality or post-rococo stiffening towards the straight lines of Neo-classicism. Most appropriately however, the chairs are covered with magnificent Régence floral tapestry, of about thirty years earlier. The chairs were probably from Wentworth Woodhouse, Yorkshire where there was an extensive suite of this design attributed to Wright and Elwick of Wakefield, Yorkshire.

Distinctly English however is fig. 96. This is a dumb waiter of about 1750

94

A very handsome Irish mahogany side table of about 1760 with a marble top, and a carved frieze with a lion mask and strong cabriole legs ending in paw feet.

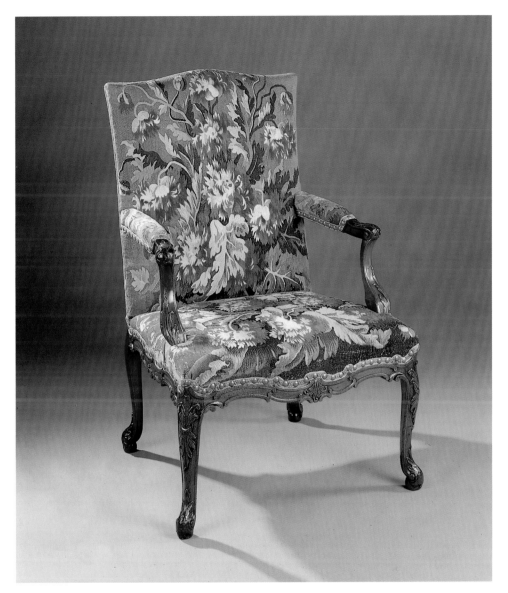

95
*One of a pair, this
mahogany armchair
of about 1760
reflects a relatively
sober rococo taste
and is covered with
fine Régence
tapestry.*

which consists of three revolving tiers on a central stem supported by a
tripod base, the three legs with double scrolls and turned up toes. Even the
rims to the tiered shelves are finely carved. A carved moulding similarly
adorns the edge of an elegant writing table of about 1765 (fig. 98). This has
straight, turned and fluted legs, a feature of the second half of the eighteenth
century when Louis XVI tastes in France and neo-classicism prevailed
across Europe. A very much larger library writing table is the Downshire
desk of circa 1770, fig. 97. Made for the centre of a room this magnificent
piece with an extravagant use of mahogany provides not only a large flat
surface for examining folios but also contains numerous drawers and a
sliding writing flap. The mouldings and ogee feet are richly carved. The
noble scale, drawing and quality of this great desk are reminiscent of the
work of William Vile.

Though it was long ago, and so we only have a black and white
photograph, shown earlier (fig. 9 on page 17), another important desk was
one of several great pieces from Rokeby Castle that passed through our
hands in 1930. This magnificent pedestal writing table is of classical

96

A mid-eighteenth century mahogany dumb waiter with revolving tiers made to hold sweetmeats and smaller dishes near a dining table.

inspiration, a form associated with William Kent and William Vile. With canted corners, all the sides are ornamented with monopoid scroll forms headed by lion masks with wings. These are linked by bandings of key pattern and vitruvian scrolls between which are panels with swags of flowers and fruit, and oval frames, all the carved details being gilded. The desk is 5 ft long. It was accompanied by an equally remarkable pair of commodes of similar classical design.

More modest but nonetheless very attractive is a smaller kneehole desk (fig. 99) with a plain wooden top edged with a beautiful gadroon moulding. This folds upwards like an architect's table and there is also a fitted writing drawer. The simple swan-neck brass handles accentuate the warm figuring of the mahogany drawer fronts on both sides.

Tall backed wing chairs, or easy chairs as they were known originally, were popular in the early eighteenth century. They had walnut legs and were rounded and cosy. Mid-eighteenth century ones, of mahogany and squarer in shape, are less common, especially when covered with spectacular needlework. The pair in fig. 100 is remarkable and was made en suite with a pair of sofas. The straight legs are decorated only with simple mouldings but the chair maker has provided a shapely frame with elegant wings and outward scrolling arms. The beautiful needlework is entirely naturalistic with, on each chair, different varieties of garden flowers growing up a blue-green trellis on a cream-white stitched background and from grassy hillocks. This furniture came from Hornby Castle and the needlework was reputedly worked by members of the Godolphin-Osborne family.

One of another pair of armchairs covered with fine needlework (fig. 102) displays more of the chairmaker's and carver's skills with noble cabriole legs and sweeping arm supports, both carved with cartouches on the knees and feet and a trailing leaf pattern from flower head paterae on the arms. The curved form of the legs reflects the rococo movement that was a crucial feature of Louis XV furniture. English furniture of the Chippendale period often combines references to this mood with more restrained classic lines that were well established here. A splendid gentleman's press of about 1765 (fig. 101) is of the finest mahogany. Its upper section has a vertical efficiency, the doors enclosing shelves for laying out clothes, while the lower part with drawers is bombé shaped and stands on ogee feet. A restrained use of carving, richly executed and with great variety, elegantly emphasises all the lines in the drawing of this piece and the ornamental brasswork decorates it without overstatement. The cabinet relates to a design for a 'Commode Clothes Press' in Chippendale's *Director*, published in 1754, plate CIV.

The choice of fine veneers shown in contrast to carving of solid timber is also shown in a chest of drawers of serpentine form (fig. 103). A pair of hall chairs (fig. 104) from Roche Court near Salisbury, Wiltshire, concentrates

97
A magnificent mahogany library table is shown in a room at our previous home in Bond Street. This great desk is richly carved and each drawer is labelled with an ivory letter. Circa 1770.

98

Representing the earlier stages of neo-classicism this writing table has straight fluted column legs but also a finely carved leaf moulding around the top edge. Circa 1765.

99

With a simple and elegant carved gadroon moulding around the top, this fine desk of about 1765 displays beautifully balanced mahogany veneering, of wonderful colour and figuring.

102

100
Chippendale period wing chairs are rarely covered in needlework. This magnificent pair from Hornby Castle are embroidered with naturalistic garden flowers growing up a trellis. Circa 1760.

entirely on sculptural forms. These chairs have a strong feeling of design, and indeed they are related to an engraving in *The Universal System of Household Furniture* by Ince and Mayhew, published between 1759 and 1763, plate IIII.

In terms of furniture, the middle of the eighteenth century is above all known for mahogany and Thomas Chippendale; and in that context chairs are generally the classic symbol. Four variations of this most familiar hallmark of English furniture (figs 105 to 108) display familiar tunes uniting the theme. All the chairs have a central splat back of vase shape, pierced and ornamented with carving. The back supports and top rails are each treated differently. Fig. 105 shows a pair of chairs that retain their original blue ground needlework. These chairs have scroll toes. The set of chairs partly shown in fig. 106 have straight plain legs, though the backs are richly drawn and carved. The armchair in fig. 107 has moulded legs joined by stretchers, while the chairs of fig. 108 (part of a set of ten chairs of which two have arms) have cabriole legs at front and back with ball and claw feet at the front and very pretty backs.

The use of walnut had not died out completely. A magnificent pair of wall brackets (fig. 109) of about 1750 displays enormous richness in rococo

101
This magnificent gentleman's clothes press combines in fine mahogany the straight forms of classic English cabinetmaking with a curvilinear lower part reflecting the rococo influence of French Louis XV furniture.

carving. Here, scrolling auricular (ear-like) shapes flow in and out lasciviously amongst leaves and flowers.

Smaller, easily moveable pieces often demonstrate a microcosm of quality and charm. A wine table (fig. 110), for example, has perfect proportions, is immeasurably handy, and with years of use has gained a superbly rich colour. It has elegant scrolling tripod legs. A noble wine cooler or plant stand (it could have been either) (fig. 113) was made in Ireland in about 1770. It has bold gadrooning around the bowl, and a solidity of construction and ornament with confident supporting legs, and hairy paw feet.

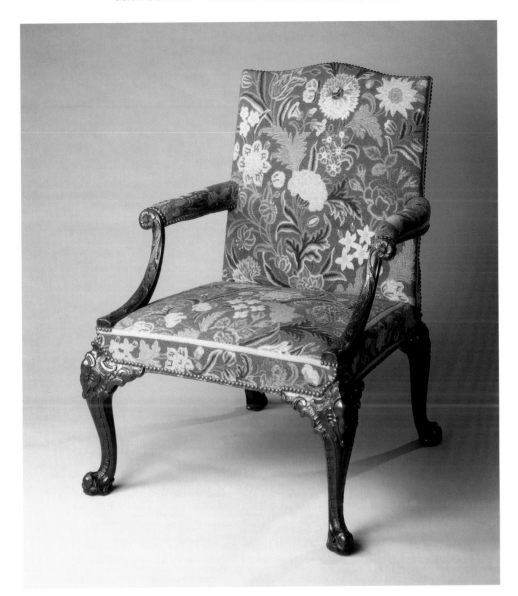

102

A splendid gainsborough or library armchair of generous scale has well carved mahogany cabriole legs and is upholstered with bright floral needlework. Circa 1765.

Silver trays and table tops shared a form of moulded pie-crust edge. This rococo pattern of contradicting flows, in both silver and wood caught the light interestingly and contrasted with the central flat surface. The table shown in fig. 111 has, typically of its type, a tripod base and a columnar stem. The top will tilt up on its side, hinged on a 'bird cage' plinth, with small pillars, that revolves on the stem. Every part of the base is most beautifully carved.

A small child's chair (fig. 112) is another smaller item of luxury furniture. The diminutive form includes many characteristic features of full-scale chairs of the 1760s. The drop-in seat could no doubt be cleaned frequently or be re-covered.

Another small masterpiece of the period is a pembroke table shown in fig. 114. Without any display of opulence this modestly proportioned table is made with extreme sophistication, every detail being superbly designed and executed with the utmost refinement. A photograph cannot convey the quality of the carved details on the legs and feet, or even the line decoration in minute parts. The delicately shaped top is crossbanded and lined around the magnificent surface veneers. The table retains its original leather castors.

103

A mid-eighteenth century serpentine fronted chest of drawers of elegant long proportions. Deep relief carving on the corners is contrasted with the mirror image veneering on the drawer fronts.

As well as for the more important requirements of furnishing, numerous smaller pieces were made for all kinds of purposes, such as a supper canterbury (fig. 115) – for the equivalent of a T.V. dinner perhaps! The pair of octagonal buckets (with modern brass liners) (fig. 116) show two aspects of rococo fantasy, pierced fret carving which was inspired by Chinese pagoda fretwork, and gothic arch shapes, a Georgian view of mediaevalism.

Returning to more substantial furnishing items, it may be noted that

104

Sculptural mahogany hall chairs almost certainly made by Ince and Mayhew, circa 1760.

105
Mahogany side chairs with pierced splat backs, scroll toes and retaining their fine original needlework seats.

collecting books and the building up of libraries was amongst the great passions of the English gentry. Fig. 117 shows one of a long series of mahogany bookcases, elegantly but simply designed to hold a great number of books around a large room – the Y label suggest that there were at least 25 such bookcases! To reach books on high shelves a stepladder was required. Fig. 118 shows a fascinating set of steps that folds as a metamorphic table. This useful double purpose would be convenient in a

106
Part of a set of chairs, two with arms sometimes known as carvers, being used at the ends of a table, though this combination is a later convention. There may have been equal numbers of side chairs and armchairs originally.

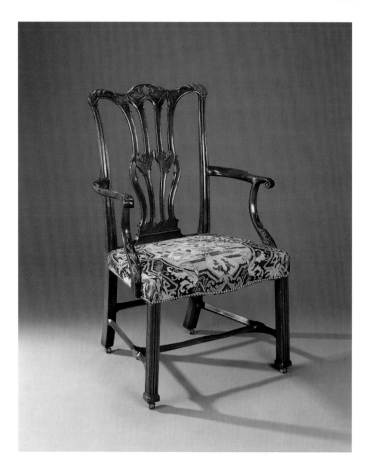

107

A Chippendale armchair with a higher back than usual. Circa 1760.

small room where one piece could perform the work of two. Equally, in a library a gentleman might wish to plan buildings and do architectural drawings, another favourite pursuit. A table for this purpose (fig. 119) which bears the stamp 'Gillows of Lancaster' is a fine example of a form that was extremely popular. This one has many handsome features, including a fold-up candle stand at the top of the raised slope, a felt-lined slide in the fitted drawer and numerous lettered compartments. You could either stand or sit at this desk.

108

Two of a set of ten chairs, two having arms, of particularly elegant form, each part shaped and ornamented. Circa 1760.

109

An occasional use of walnut continued into the mid-eighteenth century, as for these magnificently carved rococo wall brackets of about 1760.

110

A mahogany wine table of wonderful colour, on elegant scrolling legs. Circa 1770.

111

A classic and perfectly proportioned Chippendale piecrust table, the top surface contrasted with fine carving on every other part.

112

A mahogany child's chair of about 1765.

113

An Irish wine cistern or jardinière of solid mahogany, boldly carved with gadrooning and hairy paw feet. Circa 1765.

114

A superbly refined mahogany pembroke table with sophisticated detailing in carving and crossbanding in addition to the use of exceptional mahogany. Circa 1770.

A rent table would be ideal for a library or a study, perhaps in a bay window. Originally, however, these drum tables were in an entrance hall. The revolving top contained lettered drawers for the filed records of rents payable by tenants, and a well in the centre of the top was used as a cash till. Two excellent examples of these handsome drum tables with that specific purpose must be illustrated, the first (fig. 120) with a square base and with ivory letters inset into the drawer fronts. The second (fig. 121) is of a lighter, more faded mahogany and has a capstan, cylindrical base with lettering etched on satinwood inserts.

Those tables demonstrate the sensible sobriety of English furniture, the solid good taste of mid-eighteenth century English gentry. As further French and continental influences percolated this country, new fashions revolving around neo-classicism became more central to design. The next selections in my anthology of mahogany furniture reflect these. A splendid wine cooler of circa 1780 (fig. 122) is attributed to a Dublin workshop though the style dates from a time when London and Irish furniture making was closely allied. The form of this piece is clearly derived from a Roman sarcophagus; the oval form is adapted from a classical vase, while the curved fluting comes from the sides of a sarcophagus; the fan moulded top, lion mask ring handles and huge paw feet are all neo-classical features.

A splendid breakfront bookcase of the same time (fig. 123) is not of mahogany but, unusually, of yew wood. The pale warm colour and burr-like grain complement the very smooth texture of this polished timber. Severely classical in form, the bookcase is in essence in the form of a triumphal arch with central wide gate, flanked by narrower ones and is topped by a pediment, the archetypal temple end. Instead of glazing, the doors have panels of neatly twisted wire in honeycomb pattern, also reminiscent of Chinese fretwork. Tall pilasters rise up through the cabinet from the base to the fluted cornice interrupted by paterae and with further carved mouldings above. Being of native yew, much less expensive than imported mahogany and with wired doors instead of glass, this bookcase was perhaps made economically but it is now all the rarer and more special for those reasons, in addition to its exceptional qualities of proportion and workmanship.

Two more very unusual chair designs are shown in figs 124 and 125. Both are of mahogany. The first shows chairs of a fretwork form, even spider web pattern, and with cluster column legs, all vaguely Chinese in spirit. The second pair are apparently after designs by Mainwaring with lively curling

115

Small occasional tables, such as this supper canterbury were beautifully made, in mahogany, circa 1780.

116

A pair of Georgian octagonal buckets with 'gothick' pierced fretwork sides, circa 1770.

118

*A metamorphic
table, one end of
which folds open to
form a library step
ladder. Circa 1790.*

lines in the rounded escutcheon shaped backs and with, in the centre, the
shield of an unidentified baronet. The generous seats have elegant rails and
the legs are in the form of square tapering columns with fluting. A charming
urn table has some similar features (fig. 127). This occasional table would
have supported a hot water urn for making tea in the drawing room. A
small slide in the front pulls out to hold a cup. Fig. 126 illustrates one of a

117

*One of a series of
open mahogany
bookcases with
shelves of graduated
depth. Since this set
of shelves is labelled
Y it would seem that
it formed part of an
extensive library.
Circa 1790.*

119

*A handsome
'architect's desk', a
writing table with a
secretaire drawer,
for use either
standing or seated
and with an
adjustable sloping
top. By Gillows
of Lancaster,
circa 1790.*

120

A fine mahogany rent table with a revolving top, lettered drawers for records and a cash well in the top, circa 1775.

121

Another very good faded mahogany rent table, on capstan base with lettered drawers and a cash well in the top. Circa 1790.

particularly pleasing pair of English mahogany commodes in the French taste, that is of Louis XV shape with bombé sides. Representing a wholly English version of continental rococo, these chests are made from the finest mahogany and modestly charged with small carved features on the shallow aprons. This, together with the simple gilt brass mounts at the corners and on the feet gracefully emphasise an overall unity of form in a restrained and pleasing way. Again, unlike French commodes these have wood rather than marble tops. These commodes were formerly in the

122

This neo-classical wine cooler, in sarcophagus form, is based on Roman archaeological studies. It was probably made in Ireland in about 1780.

123

*An unusual neo-classical breakfront bookcase of
yew wood, finely carved and with 'chicken wire'
instead of glass in the doors. Circa 1825.*

124

Mahogany side chairs displaying distinctly English interpretations of Chinese motifs, pagoda balcony latticework in the backs and gathered 'bamboo' spindle legs.

collection of Samuel Messer who made a noteworthy collection of mahogany furniture.

Distinctly English, and a fine example of later Chippendale furniture, displaying neo-classical rather than rococo taste, is a very beautiful gentleman's clothes press of about 1765 (fig. 128). Unlike the one shown previously this is straight sided in both top and bottom sections like earlier

125

Another pair of chairs, also of about 1775, have deftly carved curved forms in the backs supporting a baronet's shield, elegant seat rails and turned tapering legs.

126

This English commode is one of a pair made in the French taste, of Louis XV bombé form, but it has a wooden rather than marble top and modest gilt metal mounts. Circa 1770.

127

Great attention has been given to detail in making this charming small piece, a stand for a hot water urn for making tea. Circa 1780.

129

One of a pair of large mahogany folding games tables with finely carved legs and mouldings. Circa 1770.

130

Another delightful card table with light flowing lines associated with the influential pattern book of George Hepplewhite. The top and edges are decorated with parquetry. Circa 1770.

128

A magnificent gentleman's clothes press of about 1765 with neo-classical features including a broken swan-neck pediment with gothic fretwork.

walnut tallboys or chests on chests. With a cupboard above, enclosing sliding shelves, and drawers below, this is of specially selected mahogany, cross-banded, and with carved and marquetry bandings. The piece has a broken swan-neck pediment with pieced gothic fretwork centred on a central plinth with a satinwood patera. It stands on ogee bracket feet. It was formerly in the Percival Griffiths collection.

I turn now to two models of card table. The first (fig. 129) shows one of a pair of large scale rectangular tables that fold open on concertina action back legs to form a square. With fine surfaces of well chosen mahogany they are ornamented all round with a classical moulding while the tall cabriole legs are carved with elongated leaves and end in scroll toes on plinths. Fig. 130 shows another card table, this one in the 'French Hepplewhite' curvilinear form associated with designs by George Hepplewhite whose book *The Cabinetmaker and Upholsterer's Guide* shows a delight in elegant forms with flowing lines, dancing cabriole legs and a sense of airiness achieved by skilful joinery and cabinetmaking. This card table has all these qualities, the solid legs and mouldings retaining a darker colour, while the marquetry veneered surfaces provide unusual contrasting shades.

Also representative of Hepplewhite is the first of a group of armchairs (fig. 131). These pretty shield back chairs, as with other successful patterns of the period, provide strength and a light appearance at the same time. Hoops and swags in the back appear to be hanging lightly, while the open arms and tapering square legs convey a sense of daintiness. A tub chair of similarly light form (fig. 132) has a more comfortable appearance with a saddle seat. The back has ribbon-like upright splats. The last two chairs are both of neo-classical form with oval backs and round tapering legs. Fig. 133 is an unusual hall chair with a curved solid back with a painted crest and

131

A pair of Hepplewhite shield back armchairs combine strength and elegance, the backs with Prince of Wales feathers and draped fabric.

garter badge, elegant curling arm supports and a solid seat (for a cushion). Fig. 134 celebrates one of the most prominent of neo-classical motifs in the back as bold decoration. This is a palmette or honeysuckle flower, wonderfully achieved in carved scrolling form. Apart from the turned legs with fluting, all the other parts are carved with a continuous laurel wreath pattern. This dignified and highly decorative chair sums up the extraordinary achievements of elegance and craftsmanship achieved in mahogany by eighteenth century chair makers.

There is however just room to show also, at the back of the book (page 356 fig. 456), an interesting recent acquisition. This is one of a pair of mahogany armchairs very similar to a well known set made for Osterley Park, Middlesex, designed by Robert Adam and made by John Linnell. Our chairs are also identical to another set on loan to Kenwood, Hampstead, from the Victoria and Albert Museum. These beautiful chairs epitomise neo-classicism with a combination of elegance and authority.

132
*A mahogany tub
chair with saddle
seat and twisted loop
uprights in the back.
Circa 1780.*

133
*This beautiful hall
chair of about 1780
has much in
common with a
Louis XVI chair
though its solid
back and seat are
unusual.
Circa 1780.*

134
*A fine late
eighteenth century
carved mahogany
open armchair, the
pattern dominated
by an archetypal
neo-classical motif, a
honeysuckle flower,
or Greek anthemion.*

Chinese Exports

―――≈≈≈≈≈❖≋≋≋≋≋―――

SHIPLOADS of commercial goods were brought to England from China by speculative traders, in the seventeenth, eighteenth and nineteenth centuries. The same goes on today, electronics and clothes for sale in Europe at very reasonable prices. But in the earlier centuries the goods were fascinatingly novel, artistic, full of life, and the expensive preserve of the rich.

Superb porcelain caused a mania in collecting and looked extremely well when massed together on a shelf or on the top of a cabinet. Queen Mary, co-ruler with William III, led a fashion in amassing fine examples, at Hampton Court and Kensington Palace. She might well have bought pieces such as a magnificent pair of vases (23½ in. tall) of the Emperor Kangxi's reign superbly decorated with panels of birds, flowers and mythical beasts in red, blue, green and yellow, shown in fig. 135. Also of the late seventeenth century are a splendid pair of blue and white jars with lids (fig. 136), decorated with scenes painted on slightly raised panels on the vases. The pointed mountains depict Chinese topography while alternate panels show different flower patterns.

A very fine Japanese export vase, 27½ in. high (fig. 137) shows a similar flower group. But this piece is of black lacquer with slightly raised gold decoration. Its elegant form and decoration owes much to China but the crisp method of decoration is distinctively Japanese. The lid has a family of chickens on it. (See also fig. 84 page 86 for another example of Japanese lacquer.)

A very rare and beautiful Japanese domed top coffer (fig. 140) dates from about 1600. It is almost 6 ft long and is entirely covered with pieces of mother of pearl in fish-scale shapes, a feature of Momoyama period decoration at its richest. The interior of the lid is decorated with panels of gilt and black lacquer. Very few large scale pieces of this kind are known to exist, but include a smaller coffer in the Victoria and Albert Museum which is similar but without the three drawers in the base.

135

A pair of tall Kangxi vases with panels of polychrome decoration including animals, birds and flowers, circa 1690.

123

136

The intensity of the blue in the painting of Kangxi vases such as these is remarkable. Alternate panels show mountains and flowers.

Amongst Chinese exports, the one that probably made the greatest impact on the interior decoration of great houses, was painted wallpaper. Many series of wallpapers were made throughout the second half of the eighteenth century and well into the nineteenth. They were traditionally used for decorating bedrooms and were sometimes complemented by painted silks or cottons for bed hangings and curtains. The European furniture for such rooms was often made in chinoiserie forms, a particularly well-known case being the bedroom at Badminton House for which Linnell and Chippendale supplied a famous pagoda bed and fretwork armchairs. Wallpapers were made of many colours with backgrounds of white or cream, brown, pink, green, blue and yellow, those last colours especially in later years. The paper was provided in vertical sheets which joined in a continuous design around the room with trees often flowing freely over the seams. Sometimes additional birds or insects were added afterwards, perhaps cut from spare pieces where doors or windows were cut out. While the subject matter was usually an out-of-doors garden or idyllic forest scene, sometimes it would instead be interior features such as shelves with books and objects, as in a

137

An elegant Japanese lacquer jar, decorated on pottery, for the export market. Circa 1720.

138
*Chinese wallpaper
was especially
favoured for
decorating
bedrooms, with
beautiful continuous
and unrepeated
designs with
flowering trees,
plants, birds and
butterflies.
Circa 1750.*

139
*Following a pattern
of the Swedish
Marieberg faience
factory these
Chinese porcelain
urns were made for
the European market
and are decorated
with an unusual
coral, and gold.
Circa 1785.*

room at Milton, Peterborough. Fig. 138 shows part of a charming Chinese exotic garden wallpaper with rocks, cranes and tropical plants.

Three more items of Chinese export porcelain must be illustrated. Two pairs of urns are interestingly based on European shapes. The first pair (fig. 139) reminiscent of baroque stone urns, of neo-classical form, are in a style of the Swedish Marieberg faience factory. Of about 1785, they are unusually decorated in coral and gilt over sculptured porcelain. On another occasion we have had a pair in blue with spiral fluting on the bases and on the lid. Secondly is a pair (fig. 141) based on a model by Josiah Wedgwood and Thomas Bentley, itself having an antique background. With 'pistol' handles these are delicately coloured with red plinths, posies in turquoise bordered oval medallions, and coral and gilded swags of husks. It is interesting to note how both these ancient European forms were revived and further adapted in China for export back to England.

A pair of standing porcelain figures (fig. 142), also Qianlong, circa 1750, represent the benevolent goddess Quan Yin, or in other eyes perhaps beautiful courtesans. With head dresses, their garments are decorated as if richly embroidered and they stand with a serene and calm pose.

The depiction of Chinese people at various activities was invariably subject enough as decorative curiosities for the European market. A fascinating painting on paper (fig. 143), probably of about 1760 shows a display of martial arts in front of a building, and watched by a troop mounted on horseback, with drummers and a row of tents behind.

I have already written about Chinese screens in the section about lacquer but here I must illustrate two more rare examples made for the export

140

A superb Momoyama period Japanese domed top coffer decorated with pieces of mother of pearl in about 1600.

141
Another pair of Chinese neo-classical style vases follow a shape adapted by Wedgwood and Bentley.

market. A most unusual one (fig. 144) was apparently made in about 1720 for the burghers of Amsterdam as it depicts a composite view of the city with several houses from different areas shown together. Presumably these were taken from engravings and a prepared drawing. The screen is made in curved form, each of the nine panels being curved horizontally and vertically as if to be placed behind the emperor's throne or that of the head of the Amsterdam civic authority. It is 8 feet wide. Somewhat later but very charming for all the life that it depicts on a red lacquer ground is a Cantonese screen of circa 1780. The side shown here (fig. 145), depicts Chinese warriors fighting in small guerrilla groups in a broad landscape of river banks dotted with pagodas.

Chinese enamel work imitated certain aspects of porcelain but the technique of painting on a metal base brought about special characteristics very different to porcelain. This work was made almost exclusively for sale to Europe and Canton was the centre of the industry. A most unusual pair of enamel dishes (figs 146 and 147) of the first part of the eighteenth century are decorated with scenes of European figures in a Chinese landscape of gardens, temples and pavilions within a hatchwork border incorporating reserves with mythological beasts. The backs of these chargers, which are 13¼ in. in diameter, are further decorated with colourful flowers and butterflies. A pair of lion-dogs (fig. 148), which support elaborate gourd-shaped vases on their heads, and lotus shaped holders for candles, were made in Canton in around 1780.

By 1770 Chinese craftsmen, encouraged by visiting English merchants, were making furniture of European forms entirely decorated with black lacquer, for export. Desks, writing tables, chairs and many smaller items were constructed fairly crudely with softwoods, heavily lacquered in black

142
Whether identified as the goddess Quan Yin or courtesans these ladies of about 1750 have a serene presence.

143
Painted on paper in about 1760 this panel depicts a display of martial arts.

144

A very rare Chinese export lacquer screen
depicting a composite view of Amsterdam, the
screen curved for placing behind a chair of
state. Circa 1720.

145

One side of a late eighteenth century
Cantonese lacquer screen shows warriors in
loose combat in a landscape, within a
dragon border.

146

A rare pair of enamel dishes with elaborate painting of scenes with European figures and mythological animals. Circa 1720.

and wonderfully decorated with gold landscapes, buildings, trees and ornamental patterns. Sometimes the decoration was of flowers in sprigs as a European would paint them, but 'chinoiserie' figures were usually not included. Fig. 149 shows a splendid bureau bookcase of this school, of a wonderfully strong design, and with shaped fronts to the lower drawers, somewhat similar to the German one illustrated on page 80. The Chinese cabinet has a grand classical pediment, between side scrolls, and over arched doors. The interiors are very much as an English one would be, but in the centre of the top part there is a wide compartment formed like a

147

The backs of the above Canton dishes are decorated with flowers and butterflies, and a geometric honeycomb.

148
*These Canton
enamel lion-dog
candlesticks of about
1780 are derived in
form from archaic
bronzes.*

Chinese shrine with pierced fret windows and trellis balconies. The outer sides of the doors and the fall front contain superb panels with mountainous, rocky and forested landscapes.

Export furniture, like porcelain, could be especially ordered for a client, with his arms or crest included in the decoration. A pair of Chinese style coffers (for which stands were made at home) were supplied to the Wyndham family from whom they passed by marriage in 1810 to the 2nd Earl of Dunraven and they subsequently went to the Dunraven seat at Adare Manor in Ireland. One is shown in fig. 153. Spectacularly beautiful watery landscapes with trees and pagodas surround roundels with the Wyndham arms on the tops and the fronts, which also have engraved brass lock plates. These are dated to the first half of the eighteenth century.

An unusual object of Cantonese lacquer is a small model paddleboat (fig. 150), which is in fact an incense burner with lidded containers at each end. On a black background the gold decoration is in two shades, one being more silvery. This includes windows in the side of the boat, a key pattern band and a vignette of two seated Chinese people under bamboo plants. This interesting object of about 1820 may have been inspired by paddle steamers working with international trading vessels anchored in the Whampoa Reach twelve miles below Canton or perhaps by an early steamer that navigated the Pearl River.

Another very beautiful art form perfected by the Chinese, and not done in England, was the mirror picture, the combination of 'reverse' painted glass pictures with mirrored backgrounds. There was a big trade in fine examples in the eighteenth century and it continued, with less quality over the next hundred years. A beautiful pair (figs 151 and 152) showed pavilions standing in lakes and a wealth of incidental details including internal furnishings, a pair of pet deer and a child flying a kite. The sky in both cases

149
*This splendidly
proportioned
Chinese bureau
bookcase made for
export imitates a
European one in
form; the
construction is
distinctly inferior
but the lacquer
decoration is
wonderful.
Circa 1760.*

150

An incense burner in the shape of a model paddle steamer. Canton, circa 1820.

151 and 152

A very fine pair of Chinese mirror pictures. Glass plates with bevelled edges were sent from Vauxhall in London to China for decoration and returned for sale to English customers. Chinese glass and mirror pictures were painted with great delicacy to formulas that included bucolic scenes, beautiful ladies in watery landscapes, animals and flowers. Circa 1760.

153

A general view and the top of one of a pair of fine export lacquer chests specially ordered with the Wyndham family arms. Circa 1740.

135

155

A Chinese painting in the European manner. One of a set of four, this shows a domestic scene with both Chinese and English style furniture.

is of mercury silvered mirror. Sadly one of these pictures was broken in transit, having survived two hundred years and the perilous original journey from China to Europe in about 1760. On the occasion of rare disasters such as this I remind myself that nothing except bronze and stone will last forever. I am glad that a picture can be published. A detail of another glass painting (fig. 154) shows a beautiful and finely dressed lady seated under a tree by a lake.

One of a series of four Chinese paintings of circa 1810 executed in oils by Youqua (fig. 155), in carved wood frames in the Chippendale manner depicts three noble ladies seated on bamboo stools at an English style tripod table and about to eat. Beyond the verandah there are pots of plants and the scene enjoys the shade of leafy trees.

This small selection of pieces made in China for export to Europe should perhaps end with two more pieces of porcelain. Firstly, I show a large punch bowl (fig. 156) of circa 1760 with ravishing *famille rose* decoration, displaying huge and richly petalled blooms of peonies in pink and red. These are seen

154

A detail of an eighteenth century Chinese mirror picture showing an elegant lady in a lakeland setting.

137

156
A magnificent large famille rose punch bowl with effulgent polychrome and gilded decoration, representative of the best of great quantities of Chinese porcelain made for the West in the middle of the eighteenth century.

above a fence of orange, which is also the dominant colour of the very elaborate border on the inside of the bowl. It is typical of the successful daring of eighteenth century decorative artists that the colours pink, red and orange were mixed. That would not normally now be considered possible. This splendid bowl is 22 inches in diameter. Secondly, and of about the same date is a richly decorated pair of jugs made perhaps for ale (fig. 157). The exceptionally comfortable shape of these provides an ideal form for very fine painting showing genre scenes with musicians, children and dogs amongst crowded domestic activity.

157
Decorated in the 'mandarin' style these fine ale jugs are painted with genre scenes. Circa 1760.

158

This beautiful painted silk panel is part of a series of late eighteenth century Chinese hangings, similar to wallpaper, with exotic birds, flowers and fruit, but in this case painted on fine cream silk.

159

*A view of a showroom with carved giltwood
furniture that includes a superb gesso
chandelier of about 1720, Kentian carved eagle
side tables, an Italian side table and French
rope stools of the nineteenth century.*

Giltwood – Eighteenth Century

———————⊰⊱———————

OUIS XIV, in setting out to create the greatest palace of all time at Versailles, ordered furniture made of precious metals, silver and gold. It was not previously unheard of – even Tutankhamun was provided for in the afterlife with chairs and tables plated with these materials. At Versailles and at other great European courts, furniture was made of silver but all too soon its monetary value had to be realised in order to finance wars and it was melted down to make money. A few rare surviving pieces remain including some in the Royal Collection at Windsor, made for Charles II and William III, and others at Knole, Kent.

Less prone to cash conversion, but in fact equally, perhaps even more spectacular, was carved wood furniture coated with plaster with further detailed carving, gilded and highly burnished. With smooth, shining and contrasted textures, this gold furniture was immensely impressive and a tradition of carved giltwood in this manner lasted well into the nineteenth century. We have learned to like it in a toned state on account of time and what we have now is not nearly as garish as it was when new. (A visit to a gilder's workshop, or indeed a brass and tortoiseshell marquetry workshop, can give an extraordinary impression of a truly historic atmosphere.)

Daniel Marot was one of the most influential French designers, and many features of his patterns percolated into English furniture including strapwork scrolls, banding patterns, lambrequins, formalised leaf patterns, masks and vases. All these are seen on a magnificent gilt carved wood and gesso centre table made in England in about 1700. This table (fig. 160), now on loan to the Metropolitan Museum, New York, may have been designed by John Gumley or James Moore. It combines some typical aspects of North European furniture design; Jacobean mannerist forms are tempered with balanced Huguenot patterns.

A fascinating pair of early wall lights in carved giltwood (fig. 161) of about 1710 are of simple form, an upright and an arm, but richly executed. The arms are of strapwork with 'breaks' in the flowing line, while the wall

160

*A magnificent
William and Mary
carved and gilt side
table with stylised
characteristics
associated with
Huguenot craftsmen
who contributed
much to English
decorative arts.*

supports, with features in common with the table described above, are
surmounted by birds, a foretaste of the creatures that invade mid-eighteenth
century giltwood furniture.

Early rococo design is exemplified in a magnificent pair of giltwood
torchères from Würzburg, Germany (fig. 162 illustrates one of them). Made
in about 1720 they combine playful and naturalistic features with earlier
formality of design. The tripod legs are of angular strapwork while the
stems are a riot of scrolls and flowers. The tops are however more formal
with ingenious carved lambrequins familiar in French Régence furniture.

An oval looking glass (fig. 163) has some of the same features with curling
strapwork and a crowned monogram at the top. Now a fine worn silver-gilt
colour, this very handsome oval mirror frame contains its original mercury
silvered glass plate which would have been very costly at the time.

By the reign of Queen Anne, English furniture had become delightfully
restrained yet perfect in detail. A folding gilt gesso card table (fig. 164) of
about 1710 has all the elegance of its time, straight turned legs with pad feet,
the frieze decorated with formalised leaves on a stamped ground, corner
roundels for candles and lambrequins below (imitating textile pelmets).

A rare and magnificent coffer of the first decades of the eighteenth century
(fig. 165) is richly decorated with the strapwork and leaf patterns derived
from designs by Jean Bérain and adapted by English gesso carvers. Many
textures are worked into the panels of pattern, while additional borders

161

*These early giltwood
wall lights, circa
1710, are of simple
form but richly
carved.*

162

*One of a pair of
German stands, for
lights or for precious
vases, show
manifestations of
rococo design but
earlier features are
also present.
Circa 1720.*

have variant bands. The stand of this chest is decorated with a Chinese key
pattern.

The *galerie des glaces* at Versailles was extraordinary for its huge quantities
of large and expensive mirror plates (almost all now replaced) and all rich
people aspired to such luxuries on a lesser scale. A pair of middle sized
Queen Anne mirrors represented here (fig. 166) have plates with gentle
Vauxhall bevelled edges which adds a dimension (impossible to photograph) to the fine giltwood and carved gesso frames. Delightfully restrained,
yet richly carved in detail, the frames have 'breaks' in the side uprights
(often marking a join in larger mirrors where it was necessary to have two
pieces of glass) and fixed crestings with semi-architectural and birds' head
scrolls centred on a central cartouche and scallop shell.

Another fine gesso mirror of about a decade later, circa 1720 (fig. 167),
has richer decoration associated with the reign of George I. With a more
elaborate outline at the top and bottom, every part of the surface of the
frame is finely ornamented with curling foliage, shells and lozenge-shaped
strapwork. On the broken pediment we notice a baroque classical feature, a
moulding of egg and dart form.

How well that mirror would look over an unusual and well carved table
that may well be Irish (fig. 168). The top is beautifully cut in the gesso with
a Bérainesque flowing overall pattern of strapwork and scrolling leaves,
while the simple shape of the piece is emphasised by a flowing apron
between winged cherub heads at the corners. These were almost certainly

143

163
This fine oval looking glass of about 1700 owes much of its design to Daniel Marot and retains its original gilding and plate.

inspired by Grinling Gibbons' carvings in the choir at St Paul's Cathedral in London. The fairly solid cabriole legs have fluting on their curved surfaces, a feature that is seen from time to time on Irish chair legs. This table was acquired in Northern Ireland.

A most interesting table of a little later, circa 1730 (fig. 169), has an interesting Irish provenance as it is known to have come from Speaker Connolly's great house, Castletown, Co. Kildare. This side table is in the classical manner, chiefly attributed in England to William Kent. Kent based his patterns on Roman forms which in turn reflected grotto shapes with plenty of sea references including fish scales on scrolling supports, as here.

164

*Games tables
entirely decorated
with carved and gilt
gesso are extremely
rare. Circa 1710.*

165

*A chest, of oriental
form, superbly
decorated with
elaborate patterns in
carved and gilded
gesso, on a
chinoiserie stand.
Circa 1715.*

One of a pair of Queen Anne gesso mirrors perhaps made to go between windows, with carved crestings that would have balanced tables below.

An early Georgian giltwood mirror has both a lively outline and superb carved gesso decoration. Circa 1720.

Classical masks, dolphins, eagles, the heads of gods and goddesses were all represented on such furniture in unity with the architectural settings that Kent cleverly devised as a whole. The pink marble top with its Sienna border is probably the original. Tables such as this often supported precious marbles which formed a significant part of collections gathered by Grand Tour travellers.

A splendid pair of torchères (fig. 173) (for lights), are in the form of classical terms whose original purpose would have been as boundary markers. These have several of the Kentian features already mentioned but may equally have been supplied by Benjamin Goodison. The archetypal caryatid form was also used for fireplaces and in other building contexts. There was great co-ordination in buildings and interior decoration during the English baroque period.

Another giltwood side table made to support a marble top (fig. 172) has again a simplicity of line ornamented cleverly in key points with sculptural features, most notably a deep shell in the centre of the apron and 'Indian' masks at the feet of the graceful legs. Indian masks, often with a cresting of feathers, feature in many forms of late seventeenth and early eighteenth century decoration and especially on Queen Anne gesso furniture.

A very rich architectural mirror (fig. 171) must be attributed to John Booker of Dublin as it has many hallmarks of his known work. These include Corinthian pillars resting on console brackets flanking the mirror

168
This rare and beautiful carved wood and gesso side table of about 1720 was almost certainly made in Ireland.

169
A carved giltwood side table in the manner of William Kent, with a bordered marble top, was originally the property of Speaker Connolly at Castletown House, Co. Kildare.

170

Of the English Paladian school associated with Burlington and Kent, this fine mirror retaining its original gilding can be attributed to Benjamin Goodison, circa 1740.

171

This fine architectural mirror is firmly attributed to John Booker of Dublin. It was probably conceived as a pier glass to hang between windows (see fig. 63).

172

A beautifully proportioned giltwood side table with cabriole legs terminating in 'Indian' heads.

These handsome stands for lights in the form of terms are attributed to either William Kent or Benjamin Goodison. Circa 1730.

Like great altar candle stands these giltwood torchères stand on tripod feet, with ornamented turned stems, and eagles support the top platform.

plate, also seen in Dublin architecture. Further characteristics are the broken pediment with classical mouldings on curves, the sanded surface enclosed below it and the richly carved frieze with a basket of flowers, ribbons and peapods. There are many bands of interesting ornament on this lovely mirror. We dated it at about 1755.

Eagles were amongst the birds and animals carved in large scale to support side tables especially around the 1730s in the tradition of William Kent (see fig. 159). Smaller ones are seen at the top of a magnificent pair of high torchères (fig. 174). Grandly baroque in scale and richness, these stands show elements derived from Renaissance bronze candle stands made for great churches, but here transposed with added mouldings and swags.

Most of the finest giltwood furniture made in the third and fourth decades of the eighteenth century was for great country houses built to emphasise the power and prestige of their owners. Sir Robert Walpole built himself a magnificent palace at Houghton in Norfolk to emphasise his authority and to establish a position of prestige. Other more ancient aristocratic families rebuilt great houses in the new Palladian style. The Wentworth family produced rival branches who competed in the building of Wentworth Woodhouse and Wentworth Castle. From the latter comes a set of armchairs almost certainly supplied by Richard Wright and Edward Elwick of Wakefield. Five of these magnificent chairs have passed through Mallett at different times. One pair is now in the Victoria and Albert Museum. Another pair is shown here (fig. 175). The fifth chair is seen in fig. 11. The giltwood frames have a rich weightiness and the carving includes the much loved fish

175

A very fine pair of giltwood armchairs made by Wright and Elwick for Wentworth Castle, Yorkshire in about 1755. They are upholstered with the original Soho tapestry.

176

These giltwood armchairs of circa 1760 in the French manner have elegant flowing lines and inward scrolling feet.

177

A massive pair of side tables, of which this is one, are nevertheless made relatively light and airy by clever rococo drawing and carving. Circa 1760.

scale motif. The chairs retain their fine original floral tapestry, which was probably woven at the Soho factory. Another handsome pair of armchairs (fig. 176) is almost identical to a set of chairs from Rudding Park, Yorkshire and perhaps came from an earlier house of the Radcliffe family. Of generous proportions, these were also once part of an extensive set. In the French taste and modestly carved, they have calm, elegant flowing lines interestingly enhanced by additional serpentine shaped seat rails.

178

One of a set of four massive carved giltwood wall brackets deeply carved with dragons curling out of rococo scrolls, attributable to a design by John Gilbert for similar brackets made for the Mansion House, City of London. Circa 1760.

179

The much loved rococo themes of grottoes, shells and mermaids is demonstrated in a giltwood wall bracket.

180

Further rococo themes, 'C' scrolls, exotic birds and chinoiserie icicles adorn another pair of wall brackets that may have supported Chinese porcelain birds.

181

The arms of this splendid mid-eighteenth century chair especially display rococo movement while the back with its gadrooned frame adds a classical element.

A pair of large marble topped side tables (fig. 177) are immensely rich in carved decoration. Despite the massive form, the details make them light and airy overall with endlessly flowing scrolls, swags, leaves and cartouches. Each feature playfully enacts the gaiety and frivolity of the rococo taste of the 1750s, though in this example we notice there is still symmetry in the design. Perfect symmetry is also maintained in a wall bracket for a clock or perhaps a sculptured bust (fig. 179). The pair of mermaids with swags of flowers, however, reflect rococo playfulness. Another pair of wall brackets (fig. 180) is dripping with chinoiserie icicles and an oriental 'pheasant' (more likely a long-necked water bird) is a ubiquitous symbol of rococo carving. Here it is framed within slightly asymmetric 'C' scrolls.

One of two remarkable giltwood rococo armchairs (fig. 181), displays extraordinary movement in the arms especially. The legs and seat rails have typical, though exceptionally carved, rococo features, while the backs are interestingly framed by gadrooned moulding, essentially a classical feature.

184

*Paired birds or
animals are
sometimes a feature
of mirror frames
made in Ireland.
This example has
several 'un-English'
features and a
fascinating irregular
scroll at the top.*

185

*Gilded and painted,
this transitional
Chippendale mirror
shows leanings
towards neo-
classicism.
Circa 1765.*

The two chairs are also curious in having distinct differences in detailing and slight variations in the proportions, though clearly they date from the same time and were made by the same workshop and probably were always together, perhaps as companion male and female versions.

It was in mirror frames that the most fanciful rococo wood carving was achieved, often with a chinoiserie flavour, especially incorporating ho-ho birds (composites of pheasants and water-birds as mentioned above), and also sometimes with other creatures, such as swans, sheep or monkeys (fig. 182) some fabulous, others domestic. Fig. 183 shows an ungilded frame of extreme delicacy with masks at either side, a feature derived from the flanking terms of earlier architectural forms. The mirror with monkeys equally has wonderful lightness and balance. Birds dive down from the top as leaf forms curl up on either side. An interesting Irish looking glass (fig. 184) has characteristically a pair of birds and between these bold and unusual 'C' scrolls. This motif is also seen at the top of a later Chippendale period gilt and painted glass of great charm (fig. 185). This oval mirror leans towards neo-classicism with a bordered oval frame ornamented with rococo flourishes and also with the ubiquitous anthemion or honeysuckle motif of ancient Greece at the base. The mirror retains its original gilding and blue green paintwork.

186

Two large wall appliques of superb carving are tentatively ascribed to designs by Thomas Johnson and the workmanship of Ince and Mayhew. A detail only is shown of the second one. They were discovered amongst surplus fittings at Burghley House and epitomise the rococo in a joyful combination of artifice and nature.

187

*Another oval
mirror appears to
be suspended in a
rope frame and is
bordered by oak
branches.
Circa 1770.*

188

*A larger mirror has
several plates
incorporated in a
clever design with
wide borders and a
towering and
graceful cresting.
Circa 1770.*

Two further mirrors are of neo-classical form, but transitional in decoration. Another oval one (fig. 187) is again framed by a double band, this time with oak branches outside a trompe l'oeil rope with a bow at the top, from which the mirror hangs gracefully. The last mirror is again bordered, this time with mirror plates behind the carving (fig. 188). This would have been placed over a side table or chimney piece. The long sweeping curves of the upper part accentuate its height and elegance, while smaller patterns charge it with finished quality. There would seem to be at least the influence of John Linnell in this design. It is 8 ft 5 in. high.

Thomas Johnson was surely the originator of the designs of a series of giltwood wall appliques, two of which are shown next in fig. 186. These were acquired from a sale of surplus items at Burghley House, Stamford, and their great quality suggests an important London maker, perhaps Ince

189
*A George II
side table richly
carved and with
strong proportions
to support a
spectacular marble
slab top.*

190
*One of a pair of
George I carved and
gilded side tables
and chairs from
Harewood House,
perhaps originally
from the Lascelles
London house, of
about 1770.*

191

*A partnership
probably created
these beautiful
chairs, the design
being Linnell's and
Chippendale the
younger being
the supplier.
Circa 1770.*

and Mayhew. These extraordinary trophies are 7 ft 4 in. high and each consists of different but complementary swags of decorative ribbons, corns, flowers and allegorical symbols.

It is unfortunately not often possible to identify the makers of fine furniture. Very little is documented and until the middle of the nineteenth century virtually no pieces were signed. The best chance of identification is house records, bills from suppliers, etc. Though it is always interesting to conjecture who the makers were, one has to be content with the fascinating

192

*In the French taste
these chairs, also of
about 1770, are in
the manner of
John Cobb.*

193
One of a great pair of Adam side tables made for 19 Arlington Street, London to a design dated 1765. Early examples of strictly neo-classical furniture, they have fine agate tops with deep borders of a Greek key pattern in white marble. These are now in the Huntington Museum, Pasadena, California.

194
Possibly designed by James Wyatt and made by Chippendale the younger are a pair of long elliptical side tables with oak leaf decoration in the marquetry on the tops and in carved giltwood on the friezes.

195
*A charming
giltwood girandole
of the Adam period
of lyre shape and
with neo-classical
ornamental features.
Circa 1780.*

196
*One of a remarkable
pair of superbly
carved neo-classical
side tables attributed
to Bonzanigo. The
very fine malachite
tops suggest they
were made by his
craftsmen when
working in
St Petersburg.*

197

*A very beautiful
oval back armchair
made to a design by
Robert Adam for
Sir Abraham Hume
in 1779.*

pursuit of tracing developments of pattern, decoration and motifs.

A pair of armchairs (fig. 191) are finely proportioned and have a ball motif on the arm ends that is associated with designs of John Linnell. The overall crispness of line and the continuous carved ornament also suggest the workshop of Thomas Chippendale the younger. It is indeed very possible that Linnell designed these chairs and that they were supplied from Chippendale's workshops in St Martin's Lane, London. Another pair of chairs (fig. 192), this time in the French taste with cabriole legs, shaped backs and flowing seat rails are equally graceful. All the edges are delicately carved with gadrooning, a feature of John Cobb's work. The upholstery coverings are of eighteenth century silver and gold brocaded silk.

In 1970 the Huntington Library and Art Gallery in California acquired a wonderful pair of neo-classical giltwood side tables, each 5 ft 6 in. long by 2 ft 6 in. (one shown in fig. 193). They have elaborate carved friezes and stand on six square and fluted legs and have beautiful marble tops of veined brown agate bordered with a Greek key pattern in white marble. Formerly the property of the Marquis of Zetland they came from 19 Arlington Street, London and were made to a design by Robert Adam dated 1765 and are attributed to Samuel Norman. These great tables now stand beneath

198

Severely neo-classical and in pure Renaissance form, this elegant pair of torchères may be attributed to James Wyatt.

199

James Wyatt is also perhaps the designer of these more distinctly English torchères with royal feathers supporting round marble tops.

Gainsborough's *The Blue Boy* and Lawrence's *Pinkie* in the Huntington Museum, Pasadena.

Fig. 194 shows one of a remarkable pair of elliptical side tables that may have been made by Thomas Chippendale the younger around 1770. They show a combination of neo-classical elements worked in both giltwood and marquetry. The finely drawn and carved legs are in the manner of James Wyatt, with deep swags of fabric, paterae and neat acanthus carving. The friezes of the two tables are most unusually applied with a realistic banding of oak leaves with acorns. The tops of the tables are of satinwood with a wide banding incorporating a guilloche pattern inset with continuous bands of oak leaves in marquetry.

A single carved giltwood girandole (wall light) (fig. 195) of about 1780 also pays respect to such architects as Robert Adam and James Wyatt. A lyre shaped mirror plate is framed with garlands of husks and appears to stand on a shelf supported by acanthus leaves. The mirror plate would reflect light from the candle arms.

Classical beyond the tastes of eighteenth century England are a magnificent pair of tables probably made by Italian craftsmen working in St Petersburg. Fig. 196 shows one of them. They are attributed to the workshops of Bonzanigo. The magnificent green malachite tops and comparable tables of similar form at Pavlosk make it likely that these were actually made in Russia. The carved ornament is of the sharpest quality, while the flower swags and gathered flowers in the urns are very deeply carved in the manner of Bonzanigo.

200

A pair of large convex mirrors, of which this is one, are enclosed by magnificently carved Garter Star frames, a bold and sure emblem of Regency England, circa 1810.

A chair made to a design by Robert Adam (fig. 197) has all the qualities of the finest late Georgian giltwood furniture. Elegantly conceived with oval back, open arms and round tapering legs, all these elements are in the form of gathered mouldings bound loosely by a continuous and spiralling thread of husks. Designs for furniture relating to this chair were drawn by Robert Adam for Sir Abraham Hume in 1779 and 1780 and are in Sir John Soane's Museum, London. The chair itself is now in The Museum of Fine Arts, Houston, Texas.

Two more pairs of torchères epitomise further aspects of the taste for neo-classicism and each is in the manner of James Wyatt. Firstly, fig. 198 shows a pair of tall stands closely following Renaissance candelabra as depicted by Raphael in pilaster paintings in the Vatican loggia. Elements and motifs are curiously but effectively piled up in tapering form. The second pair of torchères (fig. 199), are more English in feeling, with harmonious elements growing upwards from the base. The feather motif springing from a crown, at the top, is a version of the ancient badge of the Prince of Wales that was at this time a favoured emblem of decoration, honouring George III's son who was to become Regent and later King George IV. Another royal symbol, echoed in furniture design, was the Garter Star, here seen (fig. 200) as the basic form of one of a pair of large mirrors, with round convex plates. The woodwork rays forming the star points radiating from octagonal sides are superbly carved.

Mirrors

⸺⸺⟨❖⟩⸺⸺

GLASS was a luxury in the seventeenth century and mirror glass made by a mercury process that was highly poisonous, was especially precious. Louis XIV made the greatest room at Versailles a magnificent *galerie des glaces*. As mirror plates were so treasured they were frequently richly framed. I have already shown several examples in the previous chapter while considering giltwood furniture. But we can now linger a little on mirrors specifically, looking at a few more in the development of the use and presentation of these highly valued furniture items. It is curious how the precious plates justified elaborate and expensive frames, now of more interest than the glass, though it is preferable that an antique mirror has its original plates, rather than replacements.

Often having survived in some of the great country houses because they were huge and safely fixed high up on side walls, there are a number of late seventeenth century examples that we can see. Some of these are framed with further smaller plates or borders of glass and sometimes of a different colour, often with bevelled edges which catch the light to give an effect like an edge moulding. At Hampton Court Palace there are very fine pier glasses, tall mirrors in sections as large as could be made, and framed with borders and cresting plates between windows. These great glasses were frequently above tables and at night they reflected lights and resembled windows. The convention of using pier mirrors between windows continued throughout the eighteenth century. Many were designed to be above tables and the combination should be conceived as a whole. Outside palaces and great houses for which they were made and sometimes survived due to the impracticality of moving them, it is rare to find the two components together. But many such mirrors are in themselves fine pieces and others were designed to be individual and free-standing.

The grandest mirrors perhaps were those framed with eglomisé glass borders. These were of several colours, red, green or blue with gold decoration in a technique that took its name from the inventor, Monsieur

201

A magnificent red eglomisé bordered mirror attributed to John Gumley with gilt arabesque decoration and a carved cresting of strapwork. Circa 1690.

202
*Green is a
particularly rare
colour in eglomisé
decoration. This
very fine mirror is
flanked by pilasters
and has a splendid
carved cresting.*

Glom. The glass was gilded with arabesque patterns in the manner of Jean Bérain and then backed with colour in a similar method to mirror plating. This wonderful decoration was a perfect and rich foil to the brightly silvered mirror plates. John Gumley made a famous pair of such mirrors for Chatsworth, Derbyshire and may perhaps have made the superb example shown in fig. 201. This magnificent large scale mirror of about 1690 may possibly be French but English craftsmen had certainly perfected the technique and a handful of fine mirrors of the kind survive in English houses. The illustration shows a border of red gently sloping to present the central plate in cushion form. Above is a very rich cresting with elaborate gilt arabesques including mermen and winged cupids. This is enclosed within a giltwood and carved gesso strapwork frame topped with a shell.

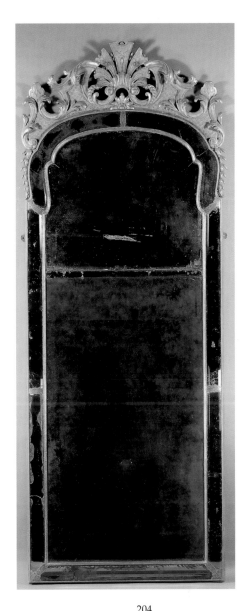

203

This William and Mary looking glass is bordered with panels of bevelled glass to catch the light and has an elaborate carved cresting that includes a full armorial achievement. Circa 1700.

204

A tall pier glass mirror of about 1700 with two large plates bordered by smaller bevelled plates and with a giltwood cresting.

Another equally magnificent eglomisé mirror (fig. 202) has green glass with pilasters at the sides also decorated with Bérainesque geometric and foliate strapwork. Again, a very rich and magnificent cresting has a wonderful decorated glass panel enclosed within a very lively frame of contradictory strapwork curves with leaves and swags and surmounted by a basket of flowers resting on a lambrequin draped plinth.

Shaped glass borders for mirrors caught the light especially when cut to interesting curves and edged with bevelling on the outsides. A fine mirror of circa 1700 (fig. 203) is framed with a mirrored border in this manner and has a very fine pierced carved cresting of tight scrolling leaves in the Dutch manner. In the centre of the cresting is a complete coat of arms with shield, helm and crest.

Fig. 204 shows an elegant pier glass of the same mirrored border type. Here the scale calls for two central plates and indeed it soon became a convention that despite size mirrors would have joined plates in this fashion. The cresting of this pier mirror is of carved giltwood and gesso with a central splayed shell motif. The joins in the border plates are of gilded paper backed with lead. A rare form of border glass mirror made in the early eighteenth century was of an upright oval, the glass border not being of

205

*Perhaps unique is
this Queen Anne
mirror with a shaped
border of black glass
with bevelled
ornamental lines.*

joined pieces but miraculously of one. Furthermore the central plate and the
border would each be bevelled evenly on the curve. Fig. 206 shows a superb
example. It has a sconce bracket at the base with a glass arm protruding
from a brass back plate.

A larger and very rare mirror from Minster House, Ripon, has a deep
border of black glass (figs 205 and 243). The central plate is framed by wide
scrolling forms with curling bevelling on the 'ears' to accentuate them and
there is a fine strapwork and broken shell cresting at the top, and glass candle
arms below.

Following the Queen Anne period mirror frames became richer with

206

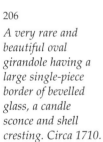

A very rare and beautiful oval girandole having a large single-piece border of bevelled glass, a candle sconce and shell cresting. Circa 1710.

207

A large Chippendale mirror made for Ramsbury Manor, Wiltshire displays interesting transitional features, rococo scrolls in the outer border and an inner frame in the neo-classical manner. Circa 1765.

elaborate carved wood ornament. I have already described a number of fine rococo examples in the previous chapter but I shall conclude here with a remarkable Chippendale mirror. 9 ft 3 in. high, this has large central plates with giltwood borders backed by mirror plates (fig. 207). The design was almost certainly by John Linnell and it is probable that the piece was made in Chippendale's workshops. It was originally at Ramsbury Manor, Marlborough. The design is especially interesting in that it marks, very successfully, the transition between florid scrolls of the rococo, as in the outer frame and the straight neo-classical inner border filled with anthemion honey suckle flowers. Two interesting Irish girandoles with oval mirrors are shown in a section on glass (see pages 321 and 322).

Furniture of the
Later Eighteenth Century

A PREVIOUS chapter described masterpieces of mahogany furniture. This one will continue with further notable pieces, together with furniture of different woods, many with marquetry. This feature became more fashionable from the middle of the century and culminated in the period of satinwood when Robert Adam and Thomas Sheraton were the most celebrated names in connection with neat neo-classical designs and spectacular cabinetmaking.

This anthology begins however with a massive mahogany library table of about 1800. This spectacular desk is shown opposite (figs 208 and 209). It has a kneehole on one side, bookshelves on the other and a concealed compartment with drawers and shelves that rides up on weighted pulleys when catches at the side are released. The top is enclosed by a brass gallery on three sides. The Bramah locks on this piece of furniture have been dated to between 1798 and 1812 by the suppliers who are still in business. The relatively plain use of timber in this large table gives it a required seriousness appropriate for a man's studies, but the form also contrasts with the more florid and fanciful furniture of the previous decades. Fig. 210 shows one of a beautiful pair of marquetry commodes which were probably made by John Cobb who had a successful furniture business with William Vile in the mid-eighteenth century. They derive their rococo shape from the even more flamboyant shapes of French commodes, but while Louis XV ones would invariably have marble tops, English commodes always had wooden tops. The other essential difference was in the use of ormolu (gilt bronze) mounts which were rarely used on English furniture, and if so, in sparing quantities. The commode shown here demonstrates fine marquetry decoration. A patterned parquetry top is inset with an oval with a large posy of flowers, while the doors on the front have graceful panels with palm leaves and elegantly hung garlands of husks tied by a ribbon, reaching across fine panels of satinwood and mahogany. Even richer is a commode by Pierre Langlois, a Frenchman who came to London and made furniture

208 and 209

A magnificent early Regency mahogany library table, 6 ft 6½ in. wide, with drawers and bookshelves and a most unusual concealed compartment in the top that rises on pulleys.

210

One of a fine pair of commodes in the French taste of satinwood and mahogany, attributed to John Cobb. Circa 1765.

for English patrons with Parisian type qualities (fig. 211). This magnificent piece of circa 1770 displays marquetry typical of this maker, finely framed within elaborate crossbanding. But it is the gilt brass mounts that are especially characteristic: an egg and dart classical moulding runs around the top, while corner mounts run from top to bottom and end in boldly scrolling toes. Also following the form of a French commode is an elegant small chest of drawers (fig. 212) with shapely legs and all sides warmly decorated with

211

A magnificent commode by Pierre Langlois who applied French characteristics to English furniture in his London workshops.

212
Another cabinet, of small size, elegantly derived from French fashions. The marquetry shows garden implements. Circa 1770.

213
English furniture is seen here to reflect a transitional Louis XVI taste with curved and floral, neo-classical and straight elements.

214

An elegant walnut pedestal desk of the mid-eighteenth century makes reference back to the beginning of the century though the form is of around 1760.

oval veneering charged with trophies of garden implements. Well placed gilt handles and small metal 'sabot' feet add a little richness. Another commode in the French taste (fig. 213) is transitional in form in that it shows a leaning towards the straight classical lines of Louis XVI furniture. The shape is essentially rectangular, but with cabriole legs (later forms being straight) and the front is finely shaped with concave and convex doors in contrasting textures inlaid with flowers. The lighter wood is harewood from the sycamore tree. The top is decorated with an urn and a long swag hung over paterae in a similar way to the one shown in fig. 210.

A curiously different writing desk (fig. 214), probably made around the middle of the eighteenth century, has old fashioned characteristics wonderfully adapted. The main wood of the veneering is walnut, but to this is added small panels of seaweed marquetry, a Dutch and English seventeenth century device. The pedestals are in a bombé form, a feature of German furniture, and the ring handles of the drawers add a Queen Anne appearance. The top is indented at the centre of each of the long sides and leathered in three parts.

A magnificent Sheraton period breakfront bookcase of large proportion is shown in fig. 215. Thomas Sheraton's *The Cabinetmaker and Upholsterer's Drawing Book* (1794) had promoted many designs including one close to that of this bookcase. Furniture associated with Sheraton's name is the epitome of fine cabinetmaking, with sensitive and restrained use of joinery and veneering at its very best. This bookcase is 9 ft 1 in. long and was formerly at Elswick Hall, Newcastle. The central section contains a secretaire drawer and the bookshelves above are enclosed behind glazed doors with fine astragal patterns of different shapes. The top cornice is decorated with a running Greek key pattern.

Three much smaller items were designed to be easily moved. An occasional table (fig. 216) of circa 1780 has delightfully flowing French Hepplewhite lines. George Hepplewhite's *The Cabinetmaker and Upholsterer's Guide* was published posthumously in 1788 greatly bolstering his reputation

as a cabinetmaker. Nothing is known certainly to have been made by him though his name, along with Sheraton's, became synonymous with the styles of much late eighteenth century furniture. The table shown in fig. 216 could be used for reading or writing and has useful screens on three sides which can be raised for protection from fire heat or draughts.

A pair of music stands (fig. 217) quite possibly by Erard's, suppliers of musical instruments and accessories, are each double sided for pairs of musicians. They have adjustable brass stems and brass arms with candle sconces. A small urn table on well spread slightly cabriole legs (fig. 218) would have supported a hot water urn or perhaps a wine cistern. The top has a gallery with rounded crenellations.

Robert Adam was of paramount importance in his influence on English neo-classical furniture. A leading architect, he took great trouble with interior decoration, and with his extensive office provided designs for every detail of each room from ceiling to carpet and from the furniture to the hardware on the doors. His devotion to the repertoire of classical ornament, which he learned in Rome and perfected to a degree of almost finicky minuteness, was developed amongst a general fashion for things reflecting

216

An occasional table in the French taste is useful for many purposes. It has vertical sliding fire or draught screens on three sides.

217

Imagine the music made around these double sided stands of about 1790.

contemporary archaeological studies in Italy. Several fine objects may be shown as indicative of that taste.

Firstly, a magnificent tambour top writing table of circa 1780 (fig. 219) shows the clean lines that were so desirable. Classical, square, tapering and fluted legs end in square plinth toes. All the mahogany veneered surfaces are richly ornamented with gilt metal mounts, each of neo-classical form: fillings in the fluted legs, swag loop handles and anthemion and husk corner brackets at the tops of the legs. An urn casket (fig. 220) of the same time achieves an equal amount of decoration in marquetry alone and with an ivory finial. An exquisite use of woods is used to depict oak leaves on the top, a coin pattern and trompe l'oeil fluting.

A fine pair of standing pedestals with lights in glass storm shades (fig. 221) display further neo-classical characteristics in terms of white paintwork and gilding on carved wood. The tapering columns are fluted with strings of husks suspended between, while this pattern gives way at the base to a double anthemion-palmette motif. Swags of drapery adorn the upper entablature. The storm shades are supported by gold lacquered brass brackets, rising to rams' heads. These pedestals were formerly at Brockenhurst Park, Hampshire.

Matthew Boulton made superb metalwork objects including numerous candelabra and urns incorporating specimens of a rare precious marble from Derbyshire, crystalline fluorspar, known as bluejohn. Three fine examples are illustrated. Fig. 223 shows two pairs of urns, one with square glass plinths, the glass panels in the manner of a speckled marble supporting vases of bluejohn with ormolu tops that turn over to form

218
This urn table was presumably at the centre of many tea parties from the 1770s onwards.

candlesticks when required. The other pair are in the form of perfume burners with pierced lids and these have white marble plinths. Each pair has finely cast and chased ormolu with many well balanced details including key pattern guilloche bands, swags of husks, elegant finials and plain lustrous surfaces. Fig. 224 shows a particularly remarkable single urn in the form of a perfume or incense burner. Here the bluejohn urn is on a double plinth, the lower one with scrolling rinceaux, while the upper one, supported by sphinxes, has sides of glass, coloured and gilt-grained on the reverse. The quality of the casting and chiselling in this case is the finest I have seen in Boulton's œuvre and I suspect that a special expert such as Benjamin Vulliamy was commissioned to carry this out. The Louis XIV style masks on the sides of the urn are especially fine. Examples of this model, less grandly executed, are in the Royal Collection.

Robert Adam at Keddleston and James 'Athenian' Stuart at Spencer House did giltwork decorations in the form of rising palm fronds. It was to this latter house that a large gilded bronze hanging lantern found its way (fig. 222). This fine lantern has four wider panes of glass in the sides, with narrower ones at the corners. The electric chandelier fitting is modern. Candles would originally have been placed on a glass bottom to the lantern.

Adam drawings would often include chimney furniture including fire grates. A further example of fine metalwork is a steel fire grate of the kind Robert Adam provided (fig. 225). This particularly interesting one has a removable front part that would not be used when the grate was in use, to simplify cleaning and in case of permanent marking. However the fixed main body is itself decorated with delicate engraving, oval paterae linked by

219
An Adam period neo-classical mahogany writing table with sliding tambour top and gilded metal mounts.
Circa 1780.

220

English woodwork alone (and an ivory finial) conveys a softer variety of neo-classical grandeur, with great refinement.

221

Late eighteenth century pedestal torchères of white and gold in the manner of Robert Adam. Circa 1780.

classical swags. This fire grate is a massive example (4 ft wide) and came from the state dining room at Wentworth Woodhouse, Yorkshire.

Turning now to masterpieces of Sheraton period furniture, I shall describe several pieces of satinwood. This light coloured wood originally came chiefly from the West Indies and was used in veneer form, laid over mahogany or other construction woods such as beech. Its golden colour and interesting grain could be used in considerable variety and in contrast to marquetry inlay and crossbanding in other woods. Sometimes it was used in solid form, but normally only for parts that could not be veneered.

A delightful oval writing table standing on four fluted legs (fig. 226) is representative of a body of relatively small pieces of furniture useful for many purposes and made with the utmost finish. A magnificent oval pembroke table of about 1775 (fig. 227) displays a superb colour and wood texture but is also very finely inlaid with tendrils of marquetry around a central shell on the top and within contrasting crossbanding with an elaborate twisted pattern.

The very important cabinet shown in fig. 228, in front of a Chinese lacquer screen of the same period, circa 1770, and with two giltwood chairs has been the subject of continued research. Similar to one other known piece, in the Metropolitan Museum, New York, it may perhaps be Irish. Alternatively, it could have been made by Christopher Fürlohg, a Swedish cabinetmaker who came to London in 1766 and worked with John Linnell but developed many individual characteristics and was cabinetmaker to the Prince of Wales. This piece is in the form of a half round commode containing a

222

A large gilt metal hanging lantern of about 1770, in the form of rising palm fronds, was acquired for the restored Spencer House.

223

Four rich and jewel-like urns supplied by Matthew Boulton in about 1780. Each of the two pairs incorporate vases of bluejohn from Derbyshire.

224

A particularly fine bluejohn urn by Matthew Boulton with ormolu mounts of exceptional quality. Circa 1780.

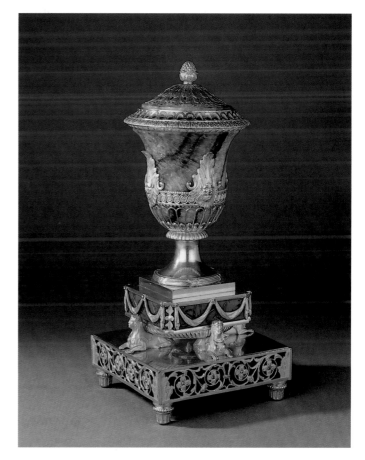

225

A massive polished and engraved steel fire grate from Wentworth Woodhouse, Yorkshire, has a removable front for safe keeping while the grate is in use.

pull-out writing compartment enclosed between curved sliding doors. Above this there is a superstructure of small drawers, a central compartment and a shelf with arched backboard supporting a small gilt bust of Bacchus. The cabinet is superbly ornamented with fine marquetry including an interesting use of wood figuring, also with fine arabesque tendrils and with oak leaves on the drawer fronts. The small drawers are locked by keyholes hidden behind small pilasters. A pictorial oval panel depicting putti on the front is derived from an engraving.

More restrained, and yet a piece of great beauty and rarity, is another pembroke table (fig. 229). This would appear to have been made by Henry Hill of Marlborough who managed to balance business between London and the fashionable town of Bath. The table has a serpentine front and back and bowed flaps. The satinwood top is laid in lozenge form with flowers in marquetry sprinkled over it.

A canterbury, originally for storing music or other folios (fig. 230) is unusually, of solid satinwood on elegant longish legs ending in brass toes and castors. Its simple lines emphasise the glorious colour of this rare and luxurious wood. Another canterbury (fig. 231), this one of mahogany and also fitted with a drawer, is decorated with a carved leaf pattern and stands on turned and reeded legs. Another rare satinwood object is a weighing machine supplied by Thomas Weekes (fig. 232) complete with small hanging scales and a set of brass weights. The woodwork is finished with fine attention to the many crossbandings and edging lines, unusual detail paid to such a utility instrument. Thomas Weekes was known for his 'Museum', a house in Tichborne Street, London where he stocked fine furniture, 'mechanical contrivances' and even stuffed birds.

Another magnificent elliptical, or demi-lune, commode (fig. 233) is attributed to Ince and Mayhew and is similar to one in the Lady Lever Art Gallery at Port Sunlight, Merseyside. Again of about 1770, this *tour de force* of English cabinetmaking is generously decorated in perfect proportion, with flowing bands of pattern with swags, ribbons, and medallions. Laurel swags on the frieze gracefully pass through paterae and drop down the

226
A late eighteenth century writing table of elegant oval form on turned and fluted legs tapering to brass castors.

227
A superb oval pembroke table of golden satinwood over which flows delicate scrolling marquetry. Circa 1780.

228

In front of a Chinese export lacquer screen is a superb cabinet, the lower part half-round and with a sliding writing compartment, the upper section with small drawers. It may have been made in Ireland.

framework towards the legs, an illusion seen in French ormolu mounts of the mid-eighteenth century.

A fine pair of folding card tables (fig. 234) have similar features to fig. 227, with floral scrolls around a large shell motif on the top surfaces. They are not large in scale and are easy to move for games, writing or eating. Larger side tables as in fig. 235 without folding tops stand taller and were not moved. This very fine example is attributed to the Dublin furniture maker, William Moore, who had previously worked with Ince and Mayhew and took neo-classicism to Ireland. Characteristic hallmarks of his work are the regularly placed honeysuckle flowers in the frieze, the harewood (stained sycamore) top and the delicate floral garland that flows round the top. Another trademark, not seen here, was regular groups of flutings around the frieze, but in this case the frieze, without that motif, is in any case especially rich in both ornament and colour.

Another very satisfactory type of table suited to many uses is the so-called sofa table, often placed behind a sofa in a large room. Longer than a pembroke table, it also has two flaps and earlier ones have end supports

229

A fine satinwood pembroke table, attributed to Henry Hill of Marlborough, circa 1780.

230

A satinwood canterbury of about 1790, for music, prints or sketchbooks.

231

It is unusual to see carved ornament on a late eighteenth century canterbury; a drawer is always a nice feature.

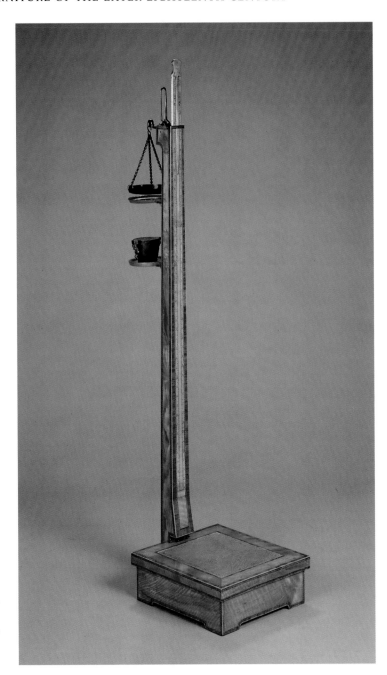

232

A very unusual
weighing machine
beautifully made in
satinwood by
Thomas Weekes.
Circa 1790.

joined by a stretcher. Fig. 236 illustrates a fine example with rosewood veneers and satinwood crossbanding. This table is fitted with a games compartment with a backgammon board concealed under a sliding top, the underside of which is marked out for draughts or chess.

A few smaller items may now be examined. Fig. 237 shows a rare octagonal satinwood wine cellaret on stand. Used for keeping bottles or decanters in, this was not for cooling, but for storage. Once again, the golden satinwood is inlaid with curling forms and marquetry resembling silk embroidery. A most unusual small table of the same time, circa 1780, is in the form of an oval box on stand (fig. 238). Perhaps for sewing silks, this table is entirely veneered in pieces of tortoiseshell with green colouring behind for the outside of the top. Ivory bandings and toes add further exotic refinement.

233
Of simple neo-classical shape, half-round, this splendid commode in satinwood has a wealth of delicate marquetry with medallions suspended on ribbons, and laurel swags.

234
A very pretty pair of late eighteenth century satinwood card tables with scrolling marquetry centred on a large shell motif.

235
William Moore of Dublin was famed for harewood, satinwood and marquetry furniture such as this beautiful elliptical side table of about 1790.

A handsome small bookcase of satinwood (fig. 239) has graded shelves above a single drawer at the base. In this instance the simple shape and rich colour are enhanced with dark ebony stringing. The rare harewood tricoteuse (a knitting, knotting, or sewing table) in fig. 241 has a fall front gallery, an applied engraving on the top and a bowed shelf below. The top, supports and legs are crossbanded with kingwood and inlaid with boxwood stringing and rosewood.

236
A fine late eighteenth century sofa table of rosewood and satinwood with a reversible top and a well with a backgammon board.

237
A charming and beautiful octagonal satinwood wine cellaret for the storage of bottles or decanters on a stand. Circa 1790.

238
A very rare small table entirely veneered with tortoiseshell, the top in the form of a box with a lifting lid, perhaps for sewing materials.

239
Golden satinwood is a rare choice of wood for a charming late eighteenth century 'dwarf' bookcase.

240

Of beautiful faded rosewood, this magnificent early Regency writing table is attributed to John McLean. With elegant brass mounts it demonstrates a perfect blend of late Georgian furniture with new classical features of the French Empire.

Rosewood was a much prized new and fashionable timber used in the last decade of the eighteenth century. It came from South America and the West Indies. The last two pieces I shall discuss here show rosewood to good advantage. A small sized drum table of about 1790 (fig. 242) has a round top with rosewood veneered drawers and a leather surface. The tripod legs are of solid rosewood (ending in brass toes and castors) while the stem is often of a less valuable but strong wood that is painted to simulate rosewood.

Perhaps the most notable maker of furniture in rosewood was John McLean whose fine writing table concludes this chapter (fig. 240). Made with mellow faded rosewood (the natural wood is very dark), the rectangular table supported like a sofa table with splayed legs at each end, joined by a turned stretcher, is glamorously ornamented with gold lacquered brasswork. Fine quality bands edge the top and drawer fronts while on the legs there are the louvre panels which are a hallmark of McLean. Another representative feature (also seen on a table by him at

Saltram House, Devon) are the trophies on the curved corners with masks and musical instruments. The lion masks on the table ends look forward to motifs of the Regency period and indeed the late Louis XVI influence and Empire taste seen in this writing table lead us very definitely into the more theatrical neo-classicism of the Regency and the early nineteenth century in general.

There was of course no sudden switch in taste and the Georgian period was to continue well into the next century, but the last years of the eighteenth century saw new European influences that broke the watertight mould of English elegance. The famed character of elegance and perfect proportions that epitomise the decorative arts in aristocratic and upper-middle class England throughout the eighteenth century were to be both enlivened and corrupted by more flashy, upstart elements reflected through military campaigns, neo-Grecian, Egyptian, and the specially staged official 'Empire' trappings of Napoleon. The mixed attitudes to such progress were not altogether unlike present feelings about European conformity.

241
This needlework table or tricoteuse is of sycamore wood (known as harewood) with an engraving on the top. Circa 1800.

242
Rosewood was the choice for a small Regency drum table but the solid stem is of another timber, painted and grained to match the rare veneers of the top and the solid rosewood legs.

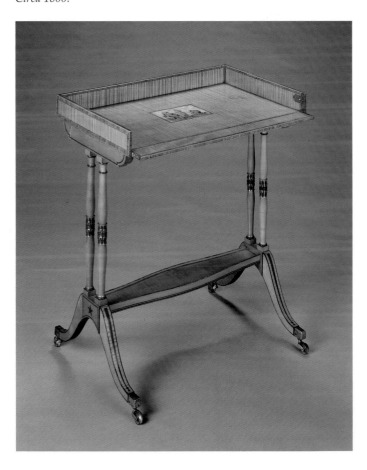

189

243

*Dominating a showroom is a gigantic round
table made in Sri Lanka in about 1830,
probably for the Governor of Ceylon.
It incorporates a great variety of exotic local
woods and stands on a solid ebony base.
(See page 194.)*

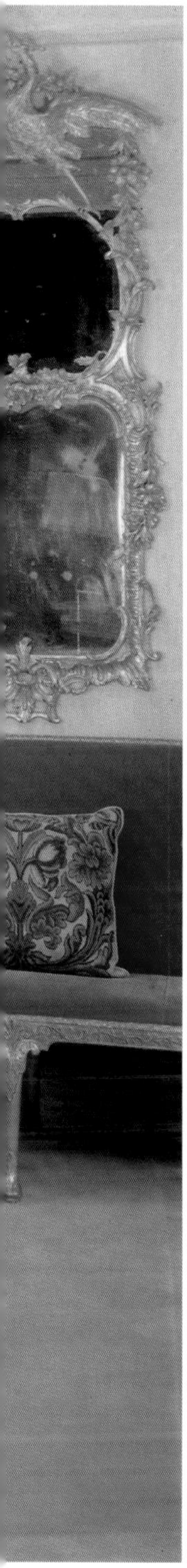

Woods

THE first two generations of English furniture, spanning mediaeval times to about 1725, used woods indigenous to Great Britain, oak and walnut. But the last two generations are chiefly known for the imported woods, mahogany and satinwood. In the earlier period limited use was also made of other local timbers such as holly and boxwood for small decorative patterns. By the eighteenth century however, a great variety of exotic materials, indeed not only woods, but ivory, tortoiseshell, mother of pearl and metals were used together with varied woods from far afield, in addition to the principal veneers of mahogany and satinwood.

This interlude between main chapters will show a few unusual uses of trees. Of the early part of the eighteenth century is an interesting small sized bureau bookcase entirely veneered with laburnum (fig. 244). With a single mirror fronted door above, enclosing book shelves, and a slope front desk below, this piece is in the Queen Anne tradition more familiar in walnut. The beautiful, strongly marked golden veneers are laid on the diagonal to achieve an interesting effect. The mirror plate is flanked by tall and thin pilasters with doric capitals carved in solid wood. The interior is of walnut.

An exquisitely made games table (fig. 246) demonstrates well the use of a wide variety of woods. The basic carcase of the top is of mahogany while the stem and legs are of solid rosewood. The top is veneered with rosewood extensively crossbanded with a broad band of another variety and finer bands of tulipwood with boxwood stringing. The backgammon interior is of leather but the reversible top has a games board of several light and dark colours including the use of speckled partridgewood. Small swing drawers on either side are constructed of cedar, still retaining its original scent after two hundred years. The drawer fronts and the legs of the table are incredibly thinly lined with boxwood stringing. This little masterpiece was made around the last decade of the eighteenth century.

Another charming use of wood is seen in a group of fruitwood tea caddies (fig. 245) made in the form of pears and a melon. Apples were also made

244

This small Queen Anne bureau bookcase is not of the expected walnut but is veneered in laburnum, a wood first used in the 1660s.

245
A melon and three pear tea caddies of fruitwood such as apple, pear or cherry. These charming little boxes would have been partly dyed with colours to look like ripe fruit but this is invariably faded.

246
Beautifully made in every detail this games table is of rosewood with satinwood and an extensive use of partridgewood for the contrasted chequerboard and other decoration. Circa 1790.

and, very occasionally, pineapples. These small lead lined boxes with locks were originally stained with colours, resembling the natural blushes of the fruit. Sometimes, as in this case, the natural and dyed colours have mellowed and developed a lovely aged tone and patination. Beware however, there are a number of fakes being made, usually dull and uniform in colour.

A very unusual Chinese card table (fig. 247) made for the export market to England is of the hardwood *huanghuali*, a wood used for Chinese

247
A Chinese export card table of the hardwood huanghuali, *with a folding top and concertina action legs at the back. Mid eighteenth century.*

These Windsor chairs, with gothic features, are typically of bent yew wood except for the seats which are usually of either ash or elm. Circa 1770.

furniture probably since antiquity. This mid-eighteenth century table of European form is carved with lion masks and paw feet and the folding interior has a border of flower and leaf patterns between guinea wells and candle stands. Another piece believed to have been made in China for an Englishman, or for export to Europe is a davenport slope top desk (fig. 249) of about 1830. Of amboyna and rosewood the top slides forward over the knees and the three drawer fronts and sides are panelled with ivory stringing. The top and slides are lined with leather. A third interesting piece (fig. 250) may also have been made in the East, perhaps in India, for a European. This is a cabinet with a secretaire drawer entirely veneered on the outside with a speckled variety of coromandel or calamander. The cabinetmaking is sophisticated which suggests that the piece could be English made (the pierced brass handles certainly are) though these veneers are not familiar.

An extraordinary table from Sri Lanka is shown opposite the opening of this short essay (fig. 243). This enormous round table (diameter 8 feet) has a top with a great variety of local woods incorporated in a large spiral pattern centred on an ivory disc engraved with the badge of the order of the Bath. Around the edge of the table is a banding of ivory incorporating a Greek key pattern. The massive and sturdy base is of solid ebony elegantly curved outwards to Regency style toes and castors of burnished and matt brass. Made in about 1830 it is believed that this magnificent table was the property of Sir Edward Barnes, Governor of Ceylon 1824–1831. A large centre table on an ebony pedestal is recorded in an inventory of his estate.

Decidedly homely however are the tavern chairs of yew tree and ash (fig. 248). These charming country chairs, Windsor chairs, have unusual gothic arched backs and gothic pierced back splats of yew. The seats are

249
A late Regency davenport of amboyna, a wood that originated in the West Indies. Circa 1830.

250
An unusual cabinet of calamander wood with a secretaire drawer. Circa 1840.

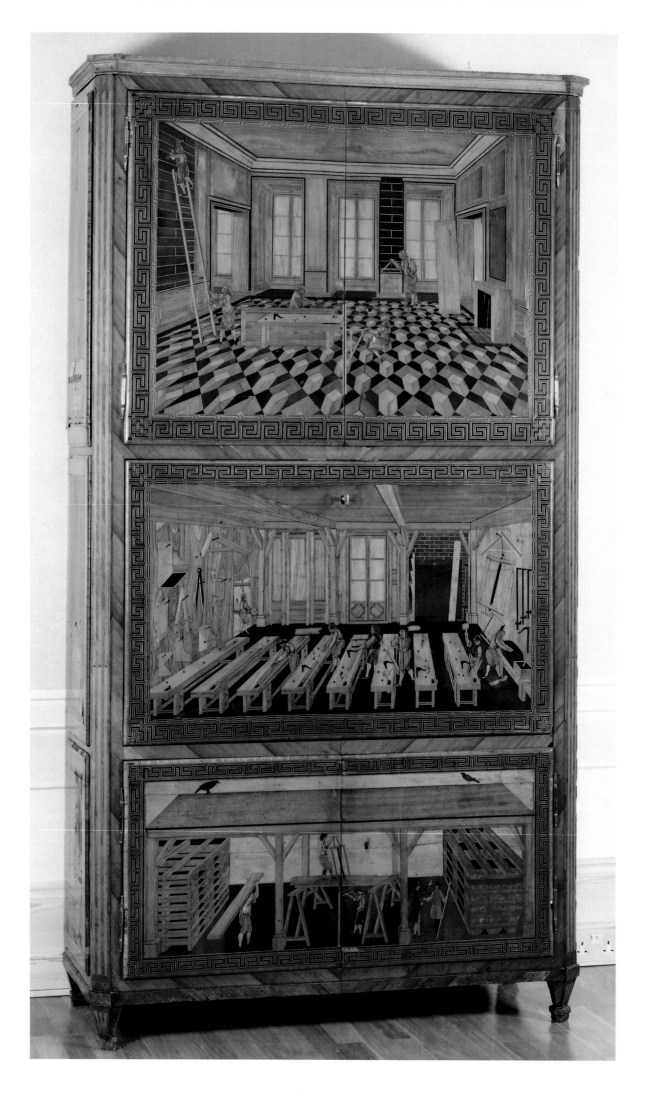

252

252

A remarkable tour de force of marquetry is seen in a nineteenth century Italian tripod table. Scenes with figures are depicted in extraordinary detail with very small pieces of wood.

251

The woodworkers depicted on this French secretaire abattant are fitting out a library and follow designs by Roubot. A fall front opens to reveal a fitted interior, the drawer fronts inlaid with specimen woods simulating a set of windows.

usually of ash or elm. The yew wood legs are cabriole shaped in the front, joined by a curved 'crinoline' stretcher.

A fascinating and unusual very tall Louis XVI secretaire abattant is shown in fig. 251. It is decorated on all three sides with marquetry showing wood-workers, following designs of 1763. A further tour de force of woodwork is a remarkable marquetry tripod table with tip-up top (fig. 252). This is thought to have been made in Sorrento, Italy in about 1840. The marquetry is of extraordinary quality, the cut shapes being very finely executed so that minute pieces of various woods portray every nuance like a painting. The technique is considerably freer than the traditional forms of marquetry, which had been inspired by *pietra dura*. Genre scenes with human figures are much more complex to portray in marquetry than are flowers, but both are successful here (fig. 252).

253

*A small dining room setting. Eight side chairs
with hoop shaped backs are drawn up around
an extending round table.*

Dining

THOUGH it was customary to dine at long tables in mediaeval times and at oak 'refectory' tables up until the seventeenth century it subsequently became the fashion for people of quality to eat, not in a great dining hall, but in the smart parade rooms. These rooms served many purposes, the most important being general promenading in fine clothes, meeting and conversation at gatherings, sitting and working (doing needlework), playing music and perhaps reading a little. In order to keep the rooms free for parading the furniture was placed around the walls and when it came to dining various small tables would be brought forward together with groups of three or four chairs at each. It was not until towards the end of the eighteenth century that long pedestal dining tables were reintroduced. Following this new arrangement in the Dining Room, sets of chairs were no longer placed around the walls but were placed along each side of the table with one at each end. A so-called set of dining chairs consisting of a number of chairs without arms and two 'carvers' (with arms) is a term of relatively modern history. Since many sets of chairs predate the dining tables they were not made in such a combination. Sets of chairs might consist of any number of armchairs and side chairs. We now take it for granted that on looking at a table surrounded by chairs, we see first the plain backs of the chairs (see fig. 253). This was because they were designed, as I have said, to be against the walls. Equally, the more elaborate front legs are now hidden under the table while we see only the much plainer back legs. Curiously the conventional manner of ornamenting chairs went on: it would have been understandable perhaps if dining chairs from around 1790 had been made with carving on their backs and with more substantial back legs!

The eight chairs in fig. 253 are related in design to those in figs 3 and 93. Here they are placed around a round mahogany table of the nineteenth century which is shown and discussed on page 203. Fig. 254 illustrates a splendid four pillar (or four pedestal) table of about 1790 with a set of fourteen Chippendale chairs of thirty years earlier, including two 'carvers',

254

A set of fourteen Chippendale chairs are here placed around an extended four pillar mahogany dining table of about 1790.

255

This fine dining table has particularly elegant pedestals, each with four legs. Extra leaves may be fitted to extend the table to double the length.

256 and 257
*Two views of a magnificent mahogany breakfast
table, one with the top folded up showing its
single piece of wood and beautiful banding.*

the twelve side chairs being without arms. The table is of solid mahogany
and the ends are rectangular with rounded corners. Each pedestal is fitted
with a tip up top for easy moving and between each of these can be placed
various combinations of leaves some wide, some narrower. Another
beautiful table (fig. 255) of much the same date has rounded D-shaped ends,
excellent width and elegant splay legs, in this case four to each pedestal.
Smaller breakfast tables seated six or eight people. Figs 256 and 257 show a
beautiful oval one of the late eighteenth century, set with Irish and English
cut glass, and showing its fine base, and also with the top folded up,
displaying the splendid mahogany timber from a tree of colossal scale, with
its fine crossbanding and line borders.

Dining rooms called for many other items of furniture in addition to
tables and chairs. Several have been seen in previous chapters but here I
can add a few more special pieces. A sideboard of about 1790 (fig. 258) is
of finely figured mahogany and the drawer fronts are decorated with fan
shaped spandrels at the corners while there are also flutings and paterae in
marquetry on the legs. A brass gallery at the back of the top would have
supported a valence to protect the wall from splashes of food, but this
feature is also derived from oak furniture where a back would support great
dishes of pewter, silver or gold. The bucket below the sideboard is Irish,
circa 1770, and was for carrying plates in and out to the kitchen. A slot down
the side enables easier access to the plates. Similar buckets without slots
were used to remove bones and scraps, but are now more often referred to
as peat buckets, another use which they were put to.

A good pair of knife boxes (fig. 259) could hold spoons and forks as well.
These have all the delicacy of neo-classical decoration of the Adam and
Sheraton period already discussed.

From Godmersham Park are a pair of Regency dumb waiters (fig. 260).
They stand on reeded mahogany tripod bases. The faded mahogany shelves
are piled on elegant brass columns and each level has a pierced brass
gallery. These tables would have held sweetmeats and been placed near the

258
A Sheraton period
mahogany sideboard
with neo-classical
marquetry and a
brass gallery.
Circa 1780.

259
A handsome pair of
knife boxes, also
with neo-classical
marquetry, of
satinwood.

260
Regency dumb
waiters provided
extra surfaces for
smaller dishes near
the dining table.
Circa 1810.

261

An early Victorian round dining table patented by Robert Jupe, with leaf extensions that fit between segments that open out on a mechanism.

dining table for easy access. In more recent times they are useful for general dining room storage or indeed in any room, especially perhaps for a collection of small objects.

Round tables usually have to be limited in size, and if large are not very stable when they have a single central support well away form diners' knees. In 1835 however, Robert Jupe of London patented an ingenious round expanding table with an iron mechanism that allowed the top to twist and open in segment form. Sets of leaves of different sizes could be inserted. Fig. 261 shows a particularly good table bearing Robert Jupe's name plates. It has two sets of leaves fitted into a handsome storage case. The wood on the table is well figured and a good colour. In its fully extended form it reaches 6 ft 9 in. in diameter.

262

A magnificent four poster bed of the Chippendale period, the front posts of mahogany, very finely carved and the shaped cresting of wood covered with silk. The portraits are by Joseph Wright of Derby.

Bedrooms

———————◆———————

O F all a man's possessions, beds were the most highly prized. Invariably early wills begin with a great bed. They were extremely expensive and made with suitable grandeur and luxury to mark the important stages of life and the continuity of prestige; birth, marriage, providing an heir and death. The life and health of the King in France was centred on the bedroom and his getting up rituals were carried out with extreme ceremony. The Lord Chamberlain still holds the highest rank in the Royal Household of Great Britain.

Almost until the advent of the Rolls Royce great beds were an ultimate status symbol and were prized for their luxury and grandeur and made with great splendour. Even by the eighteenth century they were still very prestigious and made in a very costly fashion. Mallett's have had some wonderful examples, three of which, of the second half of the eighteenth century are shown here. The first, of about 1760, is a magnificent 10 ft high four poster bed of the Chippendale period from Tabley House, Cheshire (fig. 262). The front posts are of mahogany in the form of cluster columns, very finely carved with a vertical running flower and ribbon motif and with acanthus leaves at the centre and at the base, while the square feet are also carved with acanthus and with shells. The rest of the woodwork is entirely covered with upholstery including the splendid cresting. This is of carved wood in a manner reminiscent of the great silk and velvet beds of the late seventeenth century in the style of Daniel Marot, but in this case with more of a rococo spirit. The woodcarving, as with the earlier ones, is carefully and skilfully covered with silk damask in the original manner. Before we restored this the cornice had been painted, that being a simpler option when the original fabric perished. The overall length of the bed is 6 ft 10 in. Another beautiful bed of circa 1770 (fig. 263) is partly shown in a contemporary room in Newman House, Dublin when Mallett's held an exhibition there in 1994. This fine bed has marquetry posts of mahogany inlaid with ebony and boxwood in vertical lines and a leaf pattern. The

263

Another splendid bed of about 1770, with marquetry posts and a painted cornice is partly seen here at an exhibition at Newman House in Dublin.

slightly arcaded mahogany cresting is painted with a similar leaf pattern and with a painted lambrequin cornice imitating a pelmet of embroidered silks. A third glorious bed of around 1780 is entirely painted (fig. 264). The beechwood posts and cornice are again the only wooden parts that show and these are delicately painted, originally no doubt in keeping with the hangings which may have been embroidered in a similar manner. The off-white ground of the woodwork is decorated with trailing tendrils with leaves and flowers in green, blue and red. The embroidered silk coverlet on the bed is also English of about sixty years earlier, circa 1720. Great beds

264

A very fine late eighteenth century four poster bed with carved and painted posts at the front and a painted cornice.

206

265
A mahogany bedside cabinet made in the French taste has a cupboard enclosed by tambour doors and false drawer fronts concealing a pull-out commode. Circa 1770.

266
A pair of mahogany bed steps of around 1800 are conveniently fitted with a pot and a bidet.

with deep box springs and on top of that a fat mattress are a noble height from the ground (too low a mattress on a four poster bed looks out of proportion to the design). So, to get into the bed sets of bed steps are convenient. A pair of circa 1800 (fig. 266) are of mahogany with leather treads. In each case the middle step pulls forward and contains a pot and bidet respectively. Where only bedside tables were required these usually had similar fittings. An unusual table of this kind (fig. 265) of about 1770 is made in the French taste with slightly splayed legs. A cupboard is enclosed behind a pair of concave shaped tambour doors which slide open on a mechanism, into the sides of the cabinet. The lower part, with false drawer fronts, pulls forward to reveal a commode pan.

The ultimate in travelling furniture in the early nineteenth century when military campaigns were extensively carried out all over Europe were beds of steel with gilt metal ornaments. This French 'camp' bed (fig. 267) would have been disassembled and carried with the enormous quantities of baggage that accompanied travellers in the past two centuries. It was quite normal for a nobleman or senior officer to travel with a hundred or more attendants and staff complete with carriages, wagons, horses and followers on foot.

267
An officer's campaign bed is of polished steel with gilt metal ornaments. This could be disassembled and packed for military expeditions. Circa 1810.

Clocks

⸻❖⸻

THE English perfected clock making; they devised accurate and reliable timepieces that were crucial in the successful judgement of tides, navigation and therefore world-wide travel. By the end of the seventeenth century great makers such as Thomas Tompion, Joseph Knibb, Daniel Quare, Joseph Windmills and George Graham were famed for clever and exact movements and beautifully made clocks. Charles II is said to have had forty clocks in his bedroom when he died. Understandably they have been a passion of many princes and sovereigns: a hundred years later, George III employed Sir William Chambers and others in devising great clocks.

One of the most important clock making families were the Fromanteels, originally from Amsterdam but later of London where several members were well known. Ahasuerus Fromanteel was known for fine clock cases as well as movements. A very fine large-scale musical bracket clock of circa 1700 in an ebonised case with ormolu mounts and finely engraved fretwork sides and spandrels is shown in (fig. 268). The arched dial is inscribed 'Fromanteel and Clark Amsterdam' showing their continued Dutch connections. An upper dial indicates eight tunes. This clock has an eight day movement with a going train with verge escapement, a striking train and two musical trains. That clock has an ebonised case; others were made of walnut, especially in later decades. Two splendid longcase clocks are shown. The first in fig. 269 has a marquetry case and movement by David Lestourgeon, while another with a beautiful case of walnut (fig. 270), is by John Cowell who clearly carried on the famed tradition of this wood for clock cases into the second half of the eighteenth century. The tall hood has pierced fretwork decoration to allow the sound of the bells to come through, while the face is supported by fluted columns. The long door is inset with a barometer with a gilt bezel.

Another form of decoration for early eighteenth century clocks was English lacquer, japanning. A very charming bracket clock of about 1720 by

268

A magnificent clock by Fromanteel and Clark, with eight tunes, in an ebony case and with finely engraved metalwork. Circa 1700.

269
A tall Queen Anne walnut and marquetry longcase clock profusely decorated with bird and floral inlay, the movement by 'David Lestourgeon, London'. The pair of armchairs epitomise 'Chinese Chippendale' and the chairmakers' art at its best being elegant, comfortable and strong. (See also page 16.)

Nathaniel Newman of London (fig. 271) has the delightful proportions of the times, so familiar also in Queen Anne houses. The scarlet lacquer is fabulously decorated with gold chinoiseries and the elegant lantern is topped with a large brass handle. The steel dial is marked with Arabic numerals reflecting the considerable business that was carried out by English clockmakers with Turkish buyers. By the end of the seventeenth century, trade with Turkey accounted for one quarter of all England's overseas commercial activity. Three smaller dials indicate seconds, days and strike or silent and around all the dials are gilt brass ornamental spandrels.

The French, in the eighteenth century were renowned for clock cases of ormolu rather than for movements which were simple and functional. Amongst important examples were two almost identical clocks which we have handled recently. Fig. 272 shows one of them. This magnificent

270
A beautiful eighteenth century walnut longcase clock by John Cowell with a barometer fitted in the door on the front.

271
A rare Queen Anne red lacquer bracket clock of about 1720 by Nathaniel Newman. The Arabic numerals reflect the substantial Turkish market that clockmakers supplied.

272

A superb ormolu clock of transitional style, the case by Robert Osmond, circa 1760.

273

A rare late eighteenth century Russian clock of cut steel, made at Tula, following a tradition of fine metalwork in gun making.

Louis XV clock, standing 24½ inches high has an ormolu case by Robert Osmond and movement by Le Roy of Paris, signed on the dial and the backplate. The case is stamped OSMOND on the reverse. This splendid ormolu piece, and also the second example, represent not only superb metal work of the period but a very important design in the evolution of form. This model together with a bureau plat and cartonnier belonged to Ange-Laurent Lalive de Jully being together an extremely influential suite of early neo-classical furniture, and now to be seen at the Musée Condé, at Chantilly, France. The design of the clock marks the cusp of transition between the Louis XV and the Louis XVI tastes with a sense of grandeur and heaviness redolent of Roman influence but tempered by remains of rococo decoration. The vase form was in itself a central motif in original new designs and is wonderfully successfully used as the basis for this large clock which was placed high up on the cartonnier cabinet at the top end of the writing table, in Lalive's house.

Of much the same date, circa 1770, but so very different is an English bracket clock by Eardley Norton, also with a gilt bronze case (fig. 274). Much

274

A fine English bracket clock, of about 1770, by Eardley Norton with an enamel dial and with a landscape painting above.

275

A splendid frivolity of the late eighteenth century this English ormolu clock has a playfulness and charm very different to the earlier masterpieces of English clockmakers as demonstrated in fig. 268.

less finely cast and chiselled it is nevertheless a charmingly proportioned timepiece elegantly charged with ornamental detail. The enamel face has a gentle country scene above it while spandrels, neo-classical urns, swags and mouldings make up a most pleasing overall design. Also of the late eighteenth century is a Russian cut steel mantel clock (fig. 273) made at Tula, south of Moscow, which was famous for the skill of its Imperial armouries. The steel frame is polished with a bleed sheen and is profusely decorated with diamond cut heads and clustered gilded heads, in floral and geometric forms. The enamel face has a blue border with gilt stars. The height of the clock is 14 inches.

Lastly is fig. 275, a wonderful gilt metal frivolity of the late eighteenth century attributed to James Cox. Here three enamel dials fill only a part of the face which is painted with a scene showing a couple admiring a great chinoiserie bridge by a house. The ormolu clock case includes two female figures, urns and scrolls, all on a wide plinth. Added sweetness is contributed by a bezel around the face, of blue and white glass brilliants and at the top cascades of further 'gems' in red, blue, white and yellow.

Painted Furniture

ENGLISH lacquer furniture undoubtedly represents one of the most important aspects of painted furniture and of furniture history in general. This technique of 'japanning', for the purposes of this book, has been described in a chapter of its own (page 69). But to keep this art in mind I show opposite one spectacular example (fig. 276), a Queen Anne bureau bookcase, the exterior of black lacquer and the interior of red, both richly decorated in gold chinoiseries, with use of some other colours. Such japanned pieces, being derived from imitation of Chinese lacquer, represent a very distinctive kind of painted furniture. Work of this sort was continued, with and without specific chinoiserie patterns well into the nineteenth century, and had especial favour in the Regency period. Apart from lacquer, there were in England two particularly interesting phases of painted furniture, the first around the reign of George II, epitomised by the architectural and grandiose interiors associated with Paladian architects, especially William Kent. The second was in the last thirty years of the eighteenth century when another neo-classical phase was paramount. Again with Italianate forms, this time much more defined, smaller patterns based on archaeological drawings were the rage, and the arch-priest in this school was Robert Adam. In both the Kentian and Adam periods painted furniture pays reference, even obliquely, to a stone-like or marble feeling, with cool colouring. This neo-classical appearance, in the second phase, developed into a sweeter and more colourful Sheraton form where rich golden satinwood would be decorated with brilliant flowers.

Of the earlier English Paladian type, fig. 277 shows a splendid bench with a massive architectural back in the manner of Matthew Brettingham or a contemporary. Of about 1725 this grandly elegant oak piece must have been made for a garden, an orangerie or open portico or loggia. The off-white paintwork was probably meant to approximate unpolished marble. A charming Piedmontese torchère of around 1735 (fig. 279) is in the form of a standing caryatid on a tapering plinth, and supporting a basket of flowers

276

A spectacular early eighteenth century English lacquer bureau bookcase, the outside black, the inside red, decorated with gold and coloured chinoiseries.

277

*A large oak bench
for a garden or
loggia of semi
architectural form,
painted white.
Circa 1725.*

below a dished circular top. Here the old rubbed paintwork again has a soft
stone-like appearance although originally these surfaces may have been
more like polished marbles.

Neo-classicism in English houses and furniture design could be superbly
light and lacy. A Chippendale period oval looking glass (fig. 278) has a very
finely carved horizontal frame with a fluted border edged with pearls.
Surmounting this is a large honeysuckle flower (anthemion, or palmette)
and from this swags of husks hang along the frame, balanced below by
twisted leaves. All this woodwork is painted white with highlights in green,
a scheme used on furniture made for David Garrick. A particularly
interesting and beautifully proportioned urn on stand (fig. 280) came from
Moccas Court, Herefordshire. This large piece is entirely of wood, the urn
itself being painted to simulate porphyry, and the base being stone white.
Trompe l'oeil painting was a greatly practised art in Adam decoration,
sometimes complementing real stones and marbles. Pillars and tabletops
were made of a composition to simulate semi-precious materials, especially
when large areas were impractical in the real stone. This urn, representing a

278
A Chippendale oval looking glass with a carved and painted frame, the highlights in green. Circa 1765.

279
An Italian torchère of classical form painted originally to resemble marble. Piedmontese, circa 1735.

280
An Adam carved wood urn on stand, painted to resemble porphyry, on a stone-coloured base. Circa 1780.

281
Late eighteenth century seat furniture in the neo-classical manner, with carved and painted decoration – Roman stonework translated to elegant drawing room furniture.

fine and rare quality of porphyry is an excellent example of such paintwork.

Also of the Adam period are a long stool and pair of armchairs in the English neo-classical taste (fig. 281) evolved from the Louis XVI style in France, but very individual in itself. With round tapering legs with flutings, oval backs framed with fine guilloche carving and front seat rails with small acanthus leaf decoration, all the carved surfaces and mouldings are picked out with green against the white of the frames in general. The quality of the carving is brought out in a subtle fashion, the green being in the recesses.

Less overtly classical and more English are two pairs of satinwood armchairs. Fig. 282 shows a pair with shield shaped backs while those in fig. 283 have square backs with an arcaded top rail. In both cases the seats are caned and fitted with squab cushions, the legs are square and tapering and the backs are supported by outward curving splats. The chairs are of solid satinwood, the pale colour being a luminous foil for delicate painted decoration. The painting of the shield back chairs includes realistic bunches of 'old fashioned' roses and swags, not of husks but of peacock feathers and the wood edges are trimmed in white. On the other pair the painting is more strictly neo-classical and very precise. There are however, cornucopiae filled with flowers on the uprights of the backs.

282
Satinwood shield-back armchairs of about 1790 are decorated with pretty rococo garden flowers, softening the classical lines.

283
Another pair of golden satinwood chairs are given extra colour with exquisitely painted decoration.

285

An early Victorian cabinet is lusciously decorated like oriental lacquer with gold, mother of pearl and giltwork. Circa 1845.

The chairs in fig. 282 are in the manner of George Seddon's extensive London business, the peacock feathers being a hallmark of that maker. He may also have been the supplier of a magnificent giltwood side table with a painted satinwood top, of about 1795 (fig. 284). The painting of the top is of outstanding quality and retains extraordinary freshness. The design is especially charming, with an abundance of early summer blooms in elongated cornucopiae, a central medallion of fruit framed within peacock feathers, and an outer border of bramble flowers.

The passion for flowers, lacquer and gilding all come together in a richly swagger side cabinet of about 1845 (fig. 285). The piece has a marble top and the decoration is further heightened by inset pieces of mother of pearl. The effect is complex but pretty and a fine expression of early Victorian furniture at its best.

284

A beautiful side table of circa 1795 has a satinwood top decorated with a great variety of floral and other motifs.

223

286

*One of a remarkable pair of late seventeenth
century English crewelwork bed curtains of
colourful wool embroidery on a ground of
cotton-linen twill.*

Textiles

———◆———

Just as houses today are furnished with many textiles so were they also in the past, in fact with even more and finer woven and embroidered fabrics. When we consider old sculpture, antique furniture, or any other field we tend to forget that it was accompanied by colourful and equally valued textiles. So little of the latter have survived that we have become accustomed to a museum gallery or an antiques shop with virtually no 'soft' furnishings. The wonderful treasures that I am now going to discuss a little are rare survivals of a large body of textiles that has mostly perished. Well preserved pieces are few and far between and still greatly underrated. Great beds were important possessions in larger houses. While noble families might have sumptuous beds of imported velvet or embroidered silk, lesser well-to-do households might have great beds hung with English crewelwork, wool embroidered curtains worked on homespun linen, cotton and wool. Blue, green, and more richly colourful wools were embroidered in various degrees of fineness to exotic Anglo-Indian tree of life patterns, also owing something to Flemish verdure tapestries. Fig. 286 shows a very fine example, one of a pair of large curtains of circa 1690. Originally the bed set would have had two further curtains each half the width of these, and valances. The design of these curtains was developed as a result of inter-trading through the East India Company which exported to England painted cotton palampores with related patterns. The European contribution included a wider variety of colours, domestic flowers and animals, and of course the local materials, essentially wool, the greatest national product of England. The curtain illustrated shows an undulating landscape with a chinoiserie pavilion, a stag, a spotted animal and flowers, from which grow huge vine-like trees with exotic curling leaves and branches filled with colourful birds. These curtains were formerly at Leeds Castle, Kent.

Another extremely rare form of crewelwork (fig. 287) consists of a pair of hangings worked in shades of blue wool on a fine woollen fabric.

287

Part of a very rare pair of wool embroidered hangings (see also fig. 262) to a design also done in canvaswork for chairs. Circa 1700.

In extraordinary condition, these embroideries of about 1700, are worked in satin stitch and are related to a pair of canvaswork embroidered chair seats of exactly the same pattern. This may be a unique instance of a unity of design in furnishings of different techniques. While I suspect that the previously illustrated curtains were made by amateur household embroiderers, working to supplied drawings, I think these blue embroideries were probably made in a professional workshop. Late seventeenth century chairs at Boughton House, Northamptonshire have red needlework upholstery of a similar pattern.

Embroidered pictures done in the late seventeenth century by young girls as part of their education are minor masterpieces of the English decorative arts. A small cushion of circa 1650 (fig. 288) shows one of great refinement and charm. Worked entirely in silks on satin, it depicts a well-dressed Carolean couple with a falcon between trees bearing a variety of fruit, and a

288

A mid-seventeenth century silk-embroidered small cushion, worked on satin.

lion and pond below. The embroidery is enriched with silver threads and seed pearls.

Another amateur panel (fig. 289) is a picture in glass beads sewn onto fabric and then the background dotted with shining metal spangles, each sewn on. Typical of the 1660s, it shows another courtly couple with the lady playing a lute, a pond with a great fountain, and a landscape filled with creatures, all blessed by a smiling sun.

More mature embroidery included the making of wonderful silk coverlets. A magnificent one of the early eighteenth century (fig. 290) may

289

A fine picture embroidered with coloured glass beads, the background entirely covered with spangles. English, circa 1660.

290

Still in wonderful bright condition, this Queen Anne silk coverlet is of traditional form with a central medallion, quarters at the corners and a deep border on the outside. Circa 1710.

291
An early eighteenth century silk embroidery with an exotic Anglo-Indian design on a quilted ground.

have been sewn by a young woman before she was married, or by an older relation for her. Of superb quality, this bed cover is in a conventional form, ultimately derived from Persian book bindings, where a central medallion is flanked by similar quarters, within an elaborate border pattern. Again an oriental origin is mixed with an English delicacy of ornament in a wonderfully pleasing way. Once again the condition of this textile is

292
A George I walnut sofa with its original needlework upholstery in a dense floral pattern. Circa 1720.

228

293

This magnificent French table carpet is entirely of wool, worked in vibrant colours with a black background, in about 1750.

remarkable, the silks retaining all their original shades of red, green and yellow.

A beautiful quilted panel of Queen Anne silk embroidery (fig. 291) follows further inspiration in Anglo-Indian design. Here a large and decorative 'tree of life', laden with beautiful flowers of many sorts and oriental birds, fills the frame. The work also reflects patterns of Chinese wallpaper and Indian palampores but is certainly English.

An early Georgian walnut settee (fig. 292) with six legs, finely carved in the front and with scrolling arms is upholstered with very good needlework of an all-over floral pattern. Here fully blossoming spring and summer blooms fill the ground evenly in a manner more baroque in feeling than the lightweight scrolling forms on the slightly earlier wing chair illustrated in fig. 59 page 61, for example.

Comparable in some respects, but very different in execution and effect, is a magnificent table carpet of around 1750, thought to have been made by French Carmelite nuns near Tours (fig. 293). In remarkable condition, this large piece of almost 10 ft by 7 ft 6 in. has a black ground and a very rich

294
This beautiful hanging is one of a pair made in France in about 1700, with curling leaves and exotic flowers and fruit on a cream ground.

overall pattern of leaves and flowers. The particularly beautiful border is designed to hang over the table edge showing rising plumes of feathers in bright and various shades, gathered by ribbon bows. Also French, is one of a pair of hangings, probably for walls, of circa 1700 (fig. 294). Of canvaswork, these Louis XIV panels show a densely intertwining pattern of curling leaves, exotic fruit and flowers seen against a cream coloured ground, all framed within an embroidered moulding in guilloche form.

295
*A Louis XV
needlework picture
depicting figures
employed in garden
activities by a great
architectural
fountain.*

296
*A fine English
tapestry in the
manner of
John Vanderbank
with numerous
chinoiserie vignettes
shown against a
black background.
Circa 1720.*

297

*This sampler of 1704
shows not only a
record of patterns
but also practice in
lettering including a
lengthy text.*

The stitches are in a combination of wool and silk. Each hanging is 7 ft 5 in. by 4 ft 4 in.

On a much smaller scale is a pair of Louis XV needlework pictures, probably worked from an engraving. Fig. 295 shows one of them, with a garden scene dominated by an architectural fountain, while seven figures go about various pursuits including a man picking oranges and another digging.

Returning to England, but only partially, we see a chinoiserie tapestry (fig. 296) woven in a London workshop, perhaps that of John Vanderbank in Covent Garden, in about 1720. A small number of tapestries such as this depict a combination of chinoiserie vignettes against a dark background, imitating Chinese lacquer perhaps. The result is very colourful, humorous and decorative.

Two samplers are particularly noteworthy. One dated 1704 is a band sampler, i.e. it has bands of pattern, samples as in a notebook (fig. 297). But this is interesting in that it also has lines of lettering, thereby teaching a skill to young girls that would be useful when they entered service in a great house and were required to mark linen. The lettering also forms a running text with moral overtones, a feature that gradually grew to dominate samplers to absurd and pathetic lengths in the nineteenth century. A fascinating Scottish sampler (fig. 298) commemorates the Battle of Culloden of 1746 at which the Scots, led by Bonnie Prince Charlie, grandson of

298

It is most unusual for samplers to illustrate topical events but this one commemorates the Battle of Culloden of 1746.

299

The needlework on these chairs is of a rare and beautiful early design, and demonstrates the fascination for Chinese blue and white porcelain. Circa 1710.

300

A pair of Chippendale period armchairs upholstered with magnificent pictorial needlework. Part of a set of six chairs from Stowe, Buckinghamshire.

James II, were defeated by the English army commanded by the Duke of Cumberland. The two generals were both twenty-five years old and their bloody battle was the last to be fought on British soil. The struggle, on a moor three miles east of Inverness, lasted less than an hour and the Scots were routed. Cumberland acquired the nickname Butcher Cumberland but was immortalised by Handel in his oratorio *Judas Maccabeaus* and with the chorus 'See, the conquering hero comes'. The sampler combines traditional

301

A pristine needlework seat on the top of a stool, one of a pair, which had never been used before, and also fitted with protective loose covers. Circa 1750.

302

A mid-eighteenth century embroidered picture depicting a vase of flowers with a squirrel on a brown ground.

303

A silk embroidered picture of about 1790, possibly adapted from an engraving.

elements of educational stitching with topical references including a triumphant English soldier standing over a kilted Scotsman.

A rare set of chair backs and seats (fig. 299) of the early eighteenth century show a pattern with seventeenth century blue and white Chinese pots against a red background, on dulled metal thread scrolling shelves. Related needlework is on a set of chairs at Chatsworth and a number of later versions were made, especially by Lady Victoria Weymss. These finest examples of this work however are remarkable. They have been put on modern chair frames. In 1931 Mallett's illustrated a remarkable set of six mahogany armchairs which came from Stowe, Buckinghamshire (fig. 300), the seat of the Duke of Buckingham. These have needlework coverings with large pictorial roundels depicting people engaged in rural occupations while the seats are similarly embroidered with birds and animals. It was traditional not to have human figures on chair seats, only the backs.

I show next two more charming pieces of eighteenth century canvaswork. The first (fig. 301) is one of a pair of pristine seat covers, never used before, but made in about 1750, and which we fitted to a pair of splendid walnut stools of the perfect size to take them. The superbly fresh design consists of uncomplicated but rich flowers shown against a sky blue border, while in the centres more finely worked and realistic flowers are shown against needlework of snow white freshness. The second piece (fig. 302) is a picture, possibly originally for a fire screen, showing a colourful vase full of a great variety of flowers in idealised fashion. A squirrel balances on an upper branch opposite a large moth while, below, a dove and snails are on a hillocky ground.

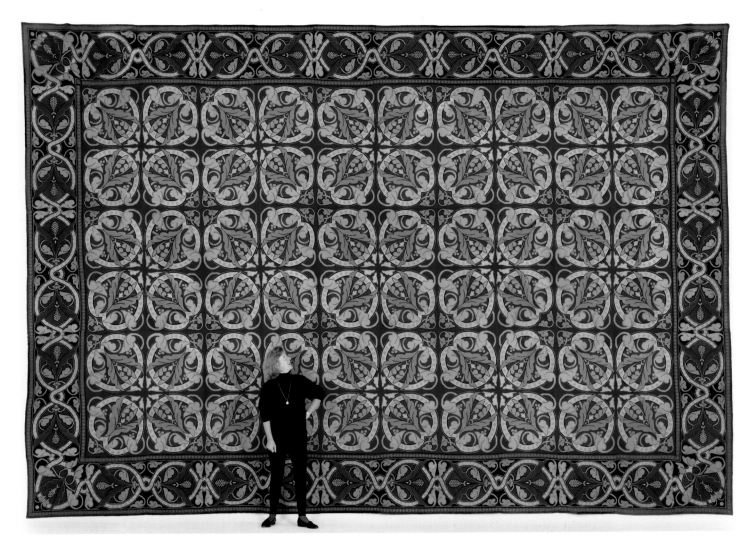

304

An enormous French needlework carpet made in squares and joined together like tiles. Circa 1850. With Paula Hunt, who is ageless.

A charming late eighteenth century silk embroidered picture (fig. 303) is the sort of piece that elegant girls 'worked' in Georgian drawing rooms and also throughout the period of Jane Austen's novels. Classical and Romantic, sometimes sentimental and even gloomy, this one shows an elegant swain placing his sweetheart's name on a tree trunk near his flock. At the opposite end of the sewing scale is a huge French carpet (fig. 304) made up of square

305

A very rare unused tapestry panel, designed and woven by William Morris for use on a sofa. Circa 1880.

306
A William Morris curtain of about 1900 (designed in 1878) with paired birds on a red ground.

'tiles' in about 1850. Again, amateur ladies would have made such useful and relatively easy needlework but the proportions of this perhaps make that unlikely in this instance. Carpets of this form were made in several countries but the design of this one is probably French.

Distinctly English however is an interesting and rare panel of tapestry designed by William Morris for use on a sofa (fig. 305). This wonderful piece was however never cut or used and is now preserved in a frame. The long scrolling leaves in blue hark back to the leaf forms of early crewelwork and of Flemish verdure tapestries while the background is covered with delicate olive green foliage on a smaller scale and pink tulips. The two small panels at the top corners were for arm pads.

Finally, fig. 306 shows a curtain of the famous bird pattern woven by the firm of William Morris with pairs of facing birds in a repeated design that had its origins in Persian textiles. This example is relatively rare, being woven in reds and pink rather than the more familiar green and blue.

European Furniture

I T is at Bourdon House that most of our French, Italian and German furniture is shown alongside many other remarkable and exciting pieces of mixed origin. One of the greatest treasures seen in recent years from France represents a great high period in furniture history, made in Paris in the reign of Louis XIV (figs 307 and 308). This remarkable commode is the pair of one in the Wallace Collection. Ascribed to Alexander Jean Oppenordt following an engraving by Jean Bérain this is a *commode en tombeau* in *contre-partie* brass and tortoiseshell marquetry, being the reverse of the *premier-partie* commode in the Wallace Collection. Both pieces have differing nineteenth century alterations but are extraordinary examples of the grandest furniture of Louis XIV's court. Made in about 1695 our commode has an oak carcase and walnut lined drawers set vertically on either side of a central drop panel in the front which conceals a black stained oak compartment. Oppenordt worked in the service of the Bâtiments du Roi and is known to have collaborated closely with Bérain in the execution of other important works for Louis XIV at Versailles and for the King of Sweden.

Another fine commode executed in the boulle technique, of circa 1700, is attributed to Nicolas Sageot (fig. 309). Of traditional form with a row of three short drawers above three long drawers (with false fronts) the spectacular top, sides and front are of Bérainesque design and mounted with richly cast lacquered mounts and handles. Again this commode is identical to a commode in the Wallace Collection except for the legs and bottom frieze. The *premier-parti* and *contre-parti* brass and tortoiseshell marquetry is of wonderful quality and closely related to similar work by Sageot in the Royal Collection in Stockholm, and other stamped pieces. The lively arabesques show playful Raphaelite fantasies as interpreted by Jean Bérain, with scrolling forms, strapwork with angular 'breaks', stylised flower forms, plumed masks, animals, birds and butterflies.

Another remarkable French item (fig. 310) is a red leather trunk of about 1740. Probably made for carrying books, this was presumably made by royal

307 and 308
This magnificent Louis XIV boulle commode is attributed to Alexander Jean Oppenordt, following a design by Jean Bérain. With very fine brass and tortoiseshell marquetry it is the pair to a commode in the Wallace Collection with marquetry in the opposite colours. Circa 1695.

309
*A fine boulle
commode attributed
to Nicolas Sageot
with brass and
tortoiseshell
marquetry in
designs associated
with Jean Bérain.
Circa 1700.*

bookbinders. It is covered in red Morocco leather with elaborate gilt tooling
and with the French royal arms, the fleurs de lys within in a lozenge
shield, denoting that it was the property of one of the unmarried daughters
of Louis XV. The sides are fitted with the original brass handles.

French provincial furniture was often very charming, with a softness of
line and mellowness in execution that is something of a relief in relation to

310
*A magnificent
Louis XV red
leather trunk
bearing the royal
arms of a daughter
of the king.
Circa 1740.*

311

A very unusual mid-eighteenth century French provincial cabinet of chestnut, with many compartments enclosed by doors.

the great riches of court furniture. Often of chestnut, a readily available indigenous wood that polishes to a warm colour similar to walnut, pieces of the Régence and Louis XV periods have pleasing rounded shapes. A remarkable and unusual example (fig. 311) is a tall cupboard with many compartments enclosed by doors. This may have been made for vestments, carefully folded and stored. Like a dresser, but fully enclosed, it stands tall but tapers towards the top a little like a chimney flue. It dates from the middle of the eighteenth century.

Another more sophisticated item is a Louis XV provincial revolving chair of walnut (fig. 312). The seat frame is very finely carved with flowers and leaves while the cabriole legs terminate in scroll toes. The revolving upper part is upholstered with the original leather. The form is like a tub or bergère chair but turning as it does on a circular frame it is possibly unique. A charming pair of Louis XV bergères (fig. 313) are tremendously welcoming

241

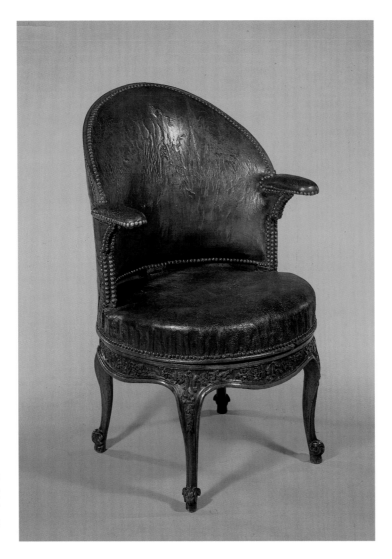

312
A rare and charming Louis XV walnut chair with a revolving seat.

313
This pair of mid-eighteenth century walnut bergères demonstrate the chairmaker's art of combining strength with an elegant lightness of line.

314

A small Chinese mirror picture in a Swedish carved giltwood frame of about 1740.

and comfortable. They are of walnut with large curved backs with a small carved flower motif at the top. With downward scrolling arms and shaped seat rails they stand on cabriole legs.

The rococo taste swept across Europe to every corner. A finely carved Swedish giltwood frame contains a very charming Chinese mirror picture (fig. 314) made in about 1740. Derived from the English early Georgian style the arcaded frame is bolder and more florid in design with a great variety of shell and flower forms, curling in and out with 'C' scrolls, on a textured and pierced ground. The Chinese mirror picture is curiously in two parts, following the convention of divided plates in larger mirrors, but otherwise a typical and delightful example of its kind. It would seem that the glass plates were made in Europe, with bevelled edges, and sent to China for the painted decoration and that the silvering was completed on their return.

Another European amalgam of influences is an Italian bureau cabinet of circa 1750 (fig. 315). This splendid piece is entirely decorated with *arte povera*

316

A splendid pair of mid-eighteenth century French ormolu candelabra in an early neo-classical manner.

317

An unusual German lacquer toilet mirror of about 1720 attributed to Gérard Dagly.

315

A fine Italian bureau cabinet, entirely decorated in the arte povera *technique, with coloured engravings glued to a painted surface, and reminiscent of European lacquer. Circa 1750.*

on a white-cream ground, in partial imitation of oriental lacquer and European japanning. It was probably made in Venice. The regularly placed motifs are printed engravings, specially made for such techniques, coloured, cut out and pasted on and then varnished. The ornate effect has all the decorative qualities of expensive porcelain and has something in common with ceramic decoration on built-in stoves covered with painted tiles.

Returning to France we see a very rich and sophisticated pair of ormolu candelabra (fig. 316). In the early neo-classical style, they follow a design by Jean-Charles Delafosse, with a notably heavy 'Roman' feeling, partly referring back to baroque classicism rather than heralding the lighter neo-classical style that was to come. This transitional mood was epitomised by designs made for Lalive de Jully (see page 214) with a noticeable presence of thick fluted columns, deep and heavy swags and stocky shapes overall. These fine candelabra have grandeur in all such novel and fashionable elements.

A black and gold lacquer toilet mirror (fig. 317) of the early eighteenth century, is thought to be German, and perhaps made by Gérard Dagly of Berlin. Dagly interestingly took his chinoiserie forms from faience and porcelain rather than from pattern books such as the English one produced by Stalker and Parker. He was a professional maker of japanned furniture, not an amateur and this lacquer he said was 'invented to delight potentates'.

Also reflecting English taste is a fine pair of gilt girandoles of about 1740 (fig. 318). Though the form of these is very much as of the reign of George I, the execution has idiosyncrasies that suggest they were made in northern

318
A fine pair of giltwood and carved gesso girandoles with mirror plates, probably Swedish, circa 1740.

319
An Italian commode, from Rome, is richly decorated with gilt and red chinoiseries on a black ground.

320

Another fine Italian commode, one of a pair, also with chinoiserie decoration, is more suggestive of porcelain, with monochrome painting in the manner of Pillement.

Europe, perhaps Sweden. The carved wood and gesso work is very fine but the drawing of the scrolls forming a broken pediment, the theatrical crown and bird crest, and the pierced cartouche wings at the base, all suggest a more unusual origin than England for these objects. The mirror plate would of course have reflected the candlelight into the room. We may now look at two beautiful painted commodes. The first (fig. 319) is a black lacquer commode with a marble top and richly decorated with gold, silver gilt and red japanning. The frieze below the two long drawers is shaped and decorated with elaborate gold patterns suggestive of rich ormolu mounts while the tall cabriole legs end in cloven hoof feet. This commode is attributed to Rome, circa 1740. The second Italian commode, one of a pair, is more like porcelain (fig. 320). Attributed to Genoa, this is also painted, but this time with a painted imitation marble top, the elaborately shaped form is white with monochrome chinoiserie decoration in the manner of Jean Pillement in coral colour. The vignettes with chinamen, pagodas and

321
*This splendid boulle bureau bookcase is
attributed to Antwerp in about 1720.
The exterior is richly decorated with brass,
tortoiseshell and mother of pearl, while the
interior is of walnut. It is flanked by Regency
torchères and there are panels of Chinese
wallpaper behind.*

towering plants are within beautifully drawn panelled borders of intricate scrolling strapwork.

A remarkable and interesting piece of furniture that crosses boundaries of date and nation, is a bureau bookcase entirely decorated on the outside with boulle, brass and tortoiseshell marquetry (fig. 321). The piece is thought to have been made in northern Europe, perhaps Antwerp, in about 1720, following the Dutch and English precedent of such cabinets. The red tortoiseshell and brass marquetry, of French inspiration, is augmented by pewter and mother of pearl, with Bérainesque figures that include cherubs, birds and winged terms. A central panel on the fall-front represents Zeus, Ganymede and Io. The interior, as would be expected of an English bureau cabinet of the early eighteenth century, is all of walnut. It is fitted with numerous compartments, drawers and pigeonholes, probably adapted later. The exterior decoration however is distinctly continental and a rich example of the boulle technique that had originated in Paris nearly half a century earlier.

322

A particularly elegant Empire writing table of mahogany with simple ormolu mounts, attributed to David Roentgen. Circa 1790.

324

*A fascinating
Charles X mahogany
boat shaped
jardinière on a tall
stand, with fine
gothic stringing in
boxwood.*

Very much calmer and a perfect expression of clean cut neo-classicism is a very fine writing table (fig. 322) attributed to David Roentgen of Neuwied, Germany, and made in about 1790. This is a *bureau à cartonnier* of fine quality mahogany with ormolu mounts in the form of louvred panels, beading and swags. A tambour front opens to reveal compartments. While Abraham Roentgen, father of David, visited England from Germany, and learned certain techniques of cabinetmaking, his son, who called himself an English

323

*A fine quality
German, or possibly
Viennese, fall-front
secretaire cabinet of
mahogany with
adjustable slides and
secret drawers.
Circa 1825.*

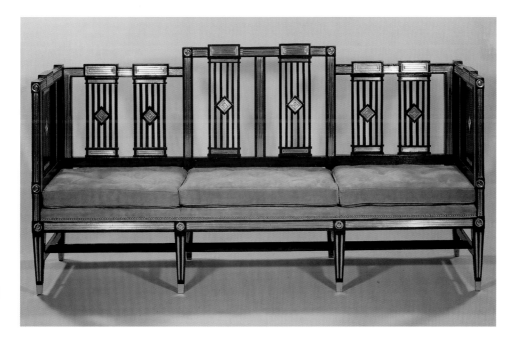

325

*An unusual Russian
mahogany and brass
sofa in the form of
multiple chairs,
made in about 1790.*

cabinetmaker moved to Paris and subsequently had considerable success in St Petersburg, making furniture for Catherine the Great. The table illustrated is amongst the finest in simple and elegant lines of all Louis XVI furniture. The angular, geometric structure of the cartonnier superstructure looks forward to the Empire style with block-like shapes and it is charmingly softened by the only curved lines, the double swag of ormolu. The round, fluted tapering legs are unusual of Roentgen's works, in which they were normally square.

A German mahogany *secretaire abattante* of circa 1825 (fig. 323) is once again of carefully selected mahogany, this time contrasted with polished brass inlay in the 'Grecian' manner and with extended caryatid pilasters, the bronze busts concealing secret pen drawers. A further hidden device, a trait of South German furniture, is a second writing slide below the top drawer which will pull forward to lean on the half opened fall front, forming a writing slope at standing height. This piece, perhaps even of Viennese origin, looks forward to the Biedermeier style, as does a most unusual Charles X jardinière of the same date (fig. 324). Presumably French in this

326

A grand yet elegant pair of small French Empire cabinets in the manner of Bernard Molitor, a German who became a registered cabinet maker in Paris. Circa 1800.

327
A pair of very charming carved and painted mirrors, probably made in Sweden. The neo-classical painting is on panels of tôle.

case, this oval boat shaped plant stand rests on a base in the form of ten columns linked by a platform stretcher at the base. The superb quality mahogany is inlaid in the gothic manner with boxwood stringing. The piece is attributed to Jean-Josse Caron the Elder, of Paris who noted that the gothic taste provided one of the mainstays of the cabinetmaking trade.

Russian furniture adopted and adapted many characteristics of furniture from further south in Europe to astonishing effect. A large quantity of modest quality seat furniture with brass moulded decoration has survived. Particularly interesting is a long mahogany sofa in this technique (fig. 325) consisting of the traditional strong neo-classical, vertical and horizontal forms, with brass bandings and fluted legs. However the scale and rhythm of the design of this piece is unusual. This massive bench was made in about 1790.

I next illustrate a very fine pair of mahogany small sized cabinets with rich ormolu mounts (fig. 326). French, circa 1805, these Empire cartonniers are in the manner of Bernard Molitor who was German by birth but moved to Paris and was received as a Maître in 1787, carrying out work for the Garde Meuble du Roi and many noble families. Like the Roentgen writing table shown above these small cabinets display a clear and jewel-like combination of well chosen mahogany veneers combined with very fine quality cast, chased and gilded mounts. They are 3 ft 6 in. high. These cabinets were sadly lost in a fire, but one hopes that others of the same form were made and have survived somewhere.

Another neo-classical item of great quality is a fine pair of painted and gilt mirrors almost certainly from Sweden; they are shown in fig. 327. The beautiful polychrome arabesques in the Etruscan taste and the ovals above, with Athena and Mars respectively, are painted on tôle. These are inset between carved giltwood mouldings and in neo-classical crestings with scrolling rinceaux, birds and baskets of flowers. Made in about 1775, it is thought that they may well have been made for the Pavilion of Gustav III at the Palace of Haga, Sweden. They are 4 ft 10 in. high.

The giltwood chairs in fig. 328 are from a famous and extensive series made in Italy, circa 1810, to a design attributed to Dionisio and/or Lorenzo Santi. There were two variant forms, one with a pointed pediment, the other with a rounded one, at the top of the back, as frequently alternated in architectural window surrounds. Large numbers of chairs, and settees, were made to these patterns but their origins remain uncertain. Cardinal Fesch,

328

Three Italian giltwood chairs, with different crestings, from a series that consisted of extended sets, made to a design attributed to Santi in about 1810. Interestingly the armchair is stamped number one.

Napoleon's uncle owned two long sets, one of each type of cresting and it is possible that he commissioned them from Santi. William Beckford also had an extensive set at Fonthill Abbey, Wiltshire, and chairs of this type also belonged to the 3rd Marquess of Londonderry at Wynyard Park, Durham, which was remodelled for this distinguished soldier and statesman by Philip Wyatt, from 1822. The chairs illustrated show both forms of cresting supported by fluted pilasters with a running husk motif beneath. Lion's paw legs support fluted seat rails.

Fig. 329 shows an interesting combination of two pieces of late neo-classical inspiration, a Charles X desk with fine marquetry in Grecian or Etruscan taste. This item was identified when we had it as being French, circa 1820. The chair however, has an interesting background. It was part of a suite of furniture designed by Filippo Pelagio Palagi for the Castello di Racconigi, Turin, a gothic revival hunting lodge belonging to King Carlo Alberto I of Sardinia. It was made in about 1850 by Gabrielle Cappello of Turin and is veneered in bird's-eye maple and mahogany on a carcase of mahogany. The chair is particularly fascinating as representing an Italian version, and late rendition of, the Empire style. Gabrielle Cappello had individual techniques in furniture making and his marquetry work in woods of contrasting colours won him a medal at the Great Exhibition of 1851.

An interesting and unusual library table (fig. 332) of about 1850 is entirely made of cedar wood and has a plate glass top in three sections above three sliding shelves. Below these are compartments for folios. This desk was designed by Alfred Jenoure of London for Sir William Stirling of Kier Mains, Perthshire as a part of a group of library furnishings. A traveller and bibliophile, Sir William had four suitable mottoes carved as an ornament around the table:

'When thou dost read a book do not turn the leaves only but gather the fruit', 'Libros y amicos pocos y buenos', 'Autant vaut celui qui chasse et rien prend comme celui qui lit et rien n'entend', 'Non v'e peggior ladron d'un cattivo libro'.

Sir William's initials are carved on one end of the desk and a group of Celtic ornaments on the other. The whole library was of cedar, a wood specially used as impervious to insect damage. This desk is learned unlike the grotto furniture below which one might call amusing. But I have learned to be cautious in using that word since the renowned Sybil, Lady Cholmondeley of Houghton Hall heard something described that way and said 'If it's amusing it isn't good. There isn't anything amusing at Houghton'.

This frivolous group of pieces (fig. 330) are Italian and were made in the late nineteenth century. These are fantasies that continue a delight in grottoes that began with the Romans or earlier, was much loved in the seventeenth century, developed in the eighteenth century into the whole taste of Rococo design, and goes on today in the form of dungeons. Slightly spooky and incorporating natural wonders brought home from the depths of the sea, real and imaginary coral and shell forms were installed in caves alongside pagan gods and goddesses. This furniture of silvery colour and knobbly textures invokes an atmosphere of moonlight and mystery, with elaborate and sometimes highly sculptural carving. With these dream-like

330

This group of late nineteenth century Italian grotto furniture is characteristic of an age-old fascination in deep sea mysteries, in shells and weird shapes.

331

A fascinating pair of marquetry armchairs in an Egyptian style with a variety of interesting veneers. Made in France, circa 1920.

nether worlds we are transported beyond England, Europe and time in playful entertainment.

From the early twentieth century, probably made in France in the 1920s is a fascinating pair of cove back armchairs (fig. 331). With cove backs these elegant chairs are a tour de force of geometric marquetry conceived in an Egyptian style and profusely inlaid with patterns in kingwood, rosewood and amaranth.

332

Made of cedar, resistant to woodworm, this library table of about 1850 was designed by Alfred Jenoure. It has a plate glass top above display shelves.

257

333

Furniture in the Chinese Room in our former premises includes a Regency rosewood drum table, one of a set of black and gold armchairs from Lord Strathmore's Gibside, Co. Durham and the 'monkey' mirror also shown in fig. 182.

The Mallett Manner

EXPENSIVE certainly, but also extremely good value. High prices are inevitably necessary if what is offered is superlative. We make it our particular business to seek out the very best and what we have is often incomparable. Naturally we depend on many other dealers in the trade to help us achieve this; we are part of a network and our speciality is to offer the finest. So we have to deal in big sums and I believe that both the rich and the less rich respect that. Our clientele includes passionate collectors with smaller means who choose to go all out to acquire truly special things.

On one occasion a notoriously grand American lady, who visited us regularly, came in. She was imperious, with a squint eye and expensively and immaculately turned out in black, being by this time a great age. Several of us nearby stood up respectfully, ready to help and she asked a director for certain things, animal pictures as it happened. She was shown some. 'I don't like any of them. What else have you got?' She was told there were more upstairs. 'Fetch 'em down and show me'. When she saw those she asked the prices of three or four, paused and turned the squint to my colleague and exclaimed 'Christ, the prices in this joint!' She bought the pictures nevertheless.

Prices nowadays are negotiable to some degree. It is a necessary convention that there is room for a discount, or a commission to agents. But when I first arrived at Mallett's, thirty years ago, as an insignificant 'squit' aged twenty-two, discussing prices was virtually unheard of. The required sum was marked clearly on the ticket, as it is today, and that was it. I remember however that it was a very distinguished Arab gentleman who taught us the technique of being flexible. We have very few Arab clients but this man was a noted and eclectic collector of fine things. Late one afternoon he admired not only a dining table but also an extensive set of white and gold armchairs that were placed around it. In a friendly manner he put his arm over my shoulder and made *an offer* for the two items. Naturally I appeared surprised and certainly could not enter into such bartering. After some time and general disappointment the client made to leave. But as he said goodbye something strangely forward in my behaviour made me take his arm and coerce him back into the shop. After 'a conversation' with my seniors a deal was concluded. That was the beginning of a new way of dealing and a new term, 'special price' was conceived.

Much more recently, I returned to the business from a City meeting and turned to matters awaiting me, on my desk. A man came into the shop and I called a junior person forward to look after him. They discussed a beautiful table in the window. After a moment the junior came back to me and said he thought I ought to speak to the client, having more knowledge. Slightly irritated, I left my work, greeted the customer and began to point out special qualities of the table. The client interrupted immediately 'Cut the bullshit! What's the price?'. Somewhat surprised I quickly calculated a 'special price' and the client walked out saying he would call me. Half an hour later he telephoned from his hotel saying he wished to buy the table; he was now extremely friendly and explained how he and his wife had stood in front of the window the previous evening, absolutely in love with the piece. We have remained good friends.

Indeed, Mallett people have built up wonderful relationships with customers, many lasting a long time. Helping clients find pieces regularly, helping build up collections and even helping make homes and fulfilling the tasks of interior decorator, have all led to special responsibilities and friendships. Francis Egerton used to tell a touching story of a late Peer, an industrialist and client who bought many fine things from Mallett. He summoned Egerton, then a young man, and asked him to arrange the decoration of his spacious London flat. Egerton enquired if the client had any particular views on the matter. He did. He sent Egerton to Southampton, telling him to go on board the *Queen Mary* and to note the decoration of the purser's lobby. This was the style he required. He had courted his wife on board that great ship and wished to commemorate that.

Husbands and wives do not always share furniture enthusiasm and sometimes indulge their passions independently. A man who bought a superb wine cooler for £12,000 was fearful of his wife's reaction and asked for this large sum not to be disclosed should she enquire. The next day they came in and the wife was cautiously shown this newly acquired treasure. She looked unmoved and said 'How much did you pay for it?' There was an awkward silence until the salesman said £1,200. '*Twelve hundred pounds?*' the wife protested, '*twelve hundred pounds!*' But the husband got away with it.

An uncertain moment in my early days occurred at lunchtime when we were relatively short staffed. It has always been customary to accompany customers around the shop, as much for courtesy and guidance as for security. On this occasion a very dapper young man in a shantung silk suit and wearing much gold jewellery came in and I took him around our rooms, noting down one or two things on a card for him. About ten minutes after he left the shop a jewellery business nearby telephoned to say that a man in a silk suit had made off with a quantity of their jewellery but had dropped our card with my name as he left. I was naturally nervous that he might have picked up loose objects at Mallett's but fortunately nothing was missing, I had been sufficiently vigilant. Unnerved after that I perhaps misjudged the next customer who happened to be untidy in appearance and was unshaven. I showed little enthusiasm and was glad when he had completed the shortest possible circuit, the ground floor only. When he got to the door he listed three things he wished to purchase which he had seen as he walked through. It turned out that he was a famous film star, growing a beard for a theatre part.

There are many stories, mostly pleasant. We have of course had plenty of petty and more serious attempts of theft, always testing and upsetting. Nowadays we have security measures, a bell on the door and a doorman so we are fortunately more relaxed inside. One lively episode with a thief made a spectacular video recording.

There have also been many characters amongst our staff but I shall recall just one, a perfect secretary of twenty-five years ago, who is sadly no longer alive. She had been brought up in Kenya and was 'colonial' in her forthrightness and her language could be colourful. Her shorthand was exquisite and she had that ability of using a spear-sharp pencil at an almost flat angle on her pad while never looking down, but gazing at the chairman or around the room as he dictated. She was a delight but maintained her own independence too, including managing to take regular puffs at a cigarette at her desk, as and when others were not looking. At lunchtime when the directors were out she took a few people through the showrooms one day and on conclusion enquired the name to which details were to be sent. 'Windsor,' she was told. 'Could you spell that please?'. It was of course the Duke. (I am sorry to say that the same fate befell Jackie Onassis who was looked after by a delightful but unsophisticated trainee.)

It was, I am sure, not that secretary to the chairman, but a younger girl whose shorthand description of table legs ended up in type describing them as standing on 'lion's poor feet'.

334

George Andrews, foreman cabinetmaker, in the restoration workshops where there are also polishers, gilders and paintwork conservators.

Great Objects

————◦◦◦◦◦◦◦◦◦◦◦————

ROOMS were always furnished with objects and textiles complementing the main pieces of furniture. Some things are perhaps neither furniture nor objects, such as barometers. A collection of these is shown opposite (fig. 335); in date these span the eighteenth century. On the extreme right is a French barometer of around 1700 (see also fig. 338); the earliest English one is a stick barometer in the manner of Daniel Quare, the case japanned in black and gold. In the centre is an elaborate Dutch barometer and thermometer of about 1770. To the left are three English barometers two with mahogany cases and the last with satinwood crossbanding and with a broken swan-neck pediment at the top. All but one of these barometers have silvered dials with elegantly engraved markings on them.

Following these beautiful instruments that reflect the furniture maker's art I shall now mention a selection of interesting objects more or less at random, though in approximate historical order. All would have enriched the rooms of rich patrons who were in a position to commission or acquire pieces of exceptional quality.

Fig. 336 shows a seventeenth century Indian box, probably for precious embroidered gloves which were greatly treasured. It is of ebony inlaid with ivory and with silver mounts which may have been provided by European traders. The *rinceaux* of alternately scrolling leaves enclosing flowers is a very ancient decorative form that had an early history in both Persia and China. This pattern is also seen on another object of much the same date, circa 1700. This is a pair of bellows (fig. 337) from Spa in Belgium, of walnut inlaid with trailing lines of brass enclosing large pieces of mother of pearl in the forms of flowers, each etched in red showing the definition of petals.

I return to further interesting instruments (fig. 338), in fact a pair, consisting of a barometer and a thermometer made in France, circa 1700. These are of ebony and green tortoiseshell, backed with green foil, or coloured on

335
A group of eighteenth century barometers, all in fine cases and ranging in date from 1700 to 1790, approximately, from right to left.

336

An Indian box of ebony and ivory with silver mounts, probably for gloves or perhaps jewels, of about 1680.

the reverse. The markings are on brass plates, finely engraved. Brass finials at the tops and small bun feet add further refinement.

An English barometer of about 1790 (fig. 339), is especially interesting for its marquetry case of satinwood, the cresting being inlaid with geometric patterns. The lozenge-shaped silvered face with brass reading needle, is surrounded by floral marquetry. The central stem is inlaid with floral marquetry and neo-classical motifs while the base has a circular mirror plate and further scrolling marquetry. There are many detailed lines of ebony and boxwood combinations that represent high quality work. It is 3 ft 10 in. tall.

337

This pair of bellows from Spa, Belgium, is of walnut inlaid with brass and mother of pearl in an Indian manner. Circa 1700.

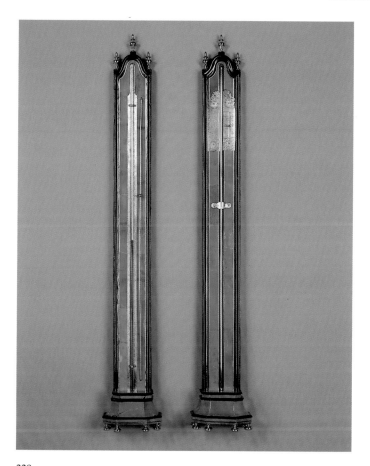

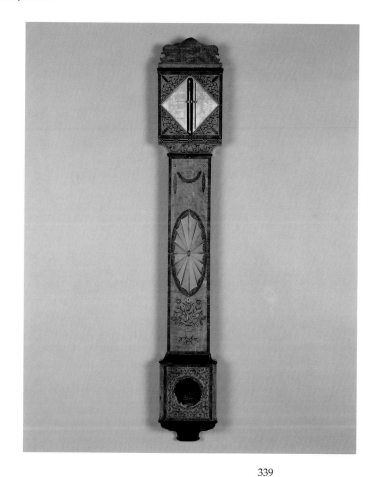

338

A beautiful pair of instruments, a barometer and a thermometer, of ebony and green tortoiseshell with brass plates. France, circa 1700.

339

A particularly beautiful late eighteenth century satinwood barometer with fine marquetry and a silvered dial.

An exotic and rich rococo object is a set of three George III silver tea caddies (fig. 343), with a pair of sugar tongs, eleven teaspoons and a mote spoon, all contained in a mother of pearl box, the silver by Edward Darville, London, 1762. The tea caddies each have rococo panels on all sides, with chinamen within arcaded buildings, and pierced chinoiserie galleries. The outer box of mother of pearl is pierced and etched and is an export piece from China, fitted in London with silver mounts, feet and a carrying handle. Tea was of course very precious in the mid-eighteenth century and so fine boxes were made for it, ready for grand ladies to supervise in drawing rooms. Another ladies' treasure is a toilet set of tortoiseshell with gold piqué decoration (fig. 340). Made in Naples in around 1760 it consists of two circular and two rectangular boxes, a small tray and a powdering brush. Each piece is inlaid minutely with pink gold piqué work of the finest quality. The decoration depicts rococo images including classical buildings, trees, birds and insects within elaborate borders of scrolling patterns and leaves.

Gentlemen were less refined. Fig. 342 shows an eighteenth century spittoon. Of mahogany, with a turned stem and carved on the bottom part, where there is a bowl under a hinged cover, which is raised by pressing the knob at the top of the pole. Men chewed tobacco and also suffered more bronchial problems than today. Spitting did not have the social stigma that it has nowadays, especially in male company. This is an interesting document of social history.

The next subject is however the height of refined elegance, a pair of Meissen swans sitting in ormolu nests and supporting three light candelabra (fig. 341). Made in about 1740, the French mounts are an early manifestation

340

A magnificent ladies' toilet set from Naples, of thick tortoiseshell inlaid with rose gold piqué.

341

A remarkable pair of Meissen swans sitting on French ormolu nests and supporting candelabra, of around 1740.

342

*A rare mahogany
spittoon, the bowl at
the base having a lid
which is opened by
pressing the knob at
the top of the pole.
Circa 1770.*

343

*This fine set of tea
caddies consists of
English chinoiserie
boxes, spoons, etc of
silver, fitted into an
elaborately cut
mother of pearl
casket from China.*

of the approaching neo-classical taste, here noticeable in the Greek key square moulded and fluted legs and also in the heavy swags. Of superb quality throughout, these candelabra have a fortunate and happy story since the mounts were found without their birds but the swans were subsequently discovered and united in their original form – one of the most beautiful objects to have passed through Mallett at Bourdon House.

Painted tôle was made in Pontypool, Wales and elsewhere in the later part of the eighteenth century and into the nineteenth. An interesting collection of green tôle objects in numerous neo-classical forms – urns, boxes, dishes, bowls and a pierced basket are partly represented in fig. 344. Each piece is of dark emerald green and has a panel with a monochrome painting resembling a neo-classical drawing, all carried out with great charm. The pieces are further decorated with foliate borders in gold.

Other very rare and unusual tôle pieces are a pair of deep rose pink pyramids (fig. 345) one of which has a removable top and inside a burner for incense. The paintwork is in wonderful original condition with floral decoration and birds, scrolling forms in shadowed gilt and there are gilt metal mounts in the form of bracket feet and pineapple finials.

An interesting group of Palais Royal oṕieces is illustrated in fig. 346. Made in Paris around 1800 and sold in shops in the vicinity of the Palais Royal these delightful sugary objects are full of fun and fantasy, rich ladies' toys of

344
A collection of neo-classical tôle urns and boxes with green and gold decoration and each with monochrome landscape scenes. Circa 1800.

the day. Ormolu of good quality and mother of pearl decorate all sorts of useful and non-essential boxes. Some contain necessaires, others musical boxes. Also displaying fine metalwork is fig. 347. Almost certainly Russian, this is another tea caddy, of cut and polished steel and with ivory mouldings and oval plaques of ivory painted with theatre scenes of the day, probably adapted from engravings of famous players. This caddy would have been safely stowed in the drawing room ready for the ceremony of tea parties.

345
An unusual pair of tôle pyramids of deep pink with coloured decoration. One contains an incense burner. Circa 1820.

346

An interesting group of Palais Royal pieces in mother of pearl with ormolu; some are useful, some are musical boxes, others simply ornamental. French, circa 1800.

347

A fine Russian cut and polished steel tea caddy with ivory bands and theatre scenes painted on ivory. Circa 1780.

348
An ormolu casket in the manner of James Cox with coloured glass resembling a rare stone. Circa 1780.

349
A fine pair of Regency globes, celestial and terrestrial, with very unusual octagonal cases probably supplied in the colonies.

350

*A magnificent large
Regency bluejohn
urn of Grecian shape
with a Wedgwood
cameo on the plinth.*

In a library would have been a good pair of table globes (fig. 349) which, in this rare instance, retain their original cases. These are domed octagonal boxes of fruitwood with brass mounts, that appear to be of colonial manufacture, perhaps made for an Englishman living abroad. The globes are a good example of a typical Regency type; they are by J. and W. Newton, 66 Chancery Lane, London. One is inscribed 'Newton's new and Improved Terrestrial Globe, published 1 July 1818' while the other has 'A New Celestial Globe' with the same date. They have turned stands of mahogany. The globes stand 22 in. high.

A beautiful casket of gilt metal (fig. 348) is in the manner of James Cox and was made in about 1780. Elaborately cast and chiselled scrolls of rococo form make up an overall square box with regularly shaped and spaced panels framing coloured glass panels, representing an exotic and unknown precious stone. Two further exhibits illustrate fine examples of real stone. The first is a large vase of bluejohn in classical urn form (fig. 350). This is made from a large piece of Derbyshire fluorspar, other examples of which are illustrated on page 179. Turned, and presented in this case in a more austere Regency manner, it displays perfectly the true translucency and crystalline nature of this wonderful semi-precious stone which can vary in

351

A superb pair of Russian malachite tazzas with ormolu dragon handles. 15½ inches high. Circa 1820.

colour considerably from deep purple to an orange-brown. The vase of Grecian shape is mounted on a plinth of lighter coloured bluejohn with a Wedgwood cameo plaque.

The second example of rare stone is a magnificent pair of malachite tazzas (fig. 351) made in Russia in about 1820. With dragon ormolu mounts, of matt and bright burnishing, these large scale urns may have been made at the Ekatarinburg lapidary works outside St Petersburg. They are veneered with

352

A very fine and rare pair of Viennese porcelain fruit coolers in the form of ancient burners, and decorated with neo-classical vignettes. Dated 1794.

353

A fine pair of Prussian porcelain urns richly decorated and with coloured panels imitating micro mosaic. Circa 1825.

pieces of malachite, carefully joined to form a consistent texture and colour. They are 17 in. in diameter and stand 15½ in. high.

Turning now to porcelain we see four fine examples, two from mainland Europe and two from England. First is a pair of Austrian fruit coolers (fig. 352). Made in Vienna and with a mark for 1794 these exceptional standing urns are in the neo-classical form of Antique burners, standing on tall legs and with pierced covers. Standing 17½ in. high they are decorated in geometric divisions with a great variety of neo-classical sculptural and ornamental patterns in both 'grisaille' and gilt, on a mauve ground. Inspired in large part by recent excavations in Pompeii, these represent gloriously the more austere neo-classicism that was the hallmark of the Empire period and which became dominant in European taste.

From Berlin is a very fine pair of Prussian vases of about 1825 (fig. 353). Again of classical form (as in the archetypal Medici vase), these are very richly and perfectly gilded in contrasting tones and textures and they stand on simulated lapis lazuli bases. But of greatest interest are the pictorial reserves on each side in the form of imitation micro-mosaics depicting doves, swans and a hound. The vases were made in the very successful Berlin Porcelain Manufactory in the reign of Friedrich Wilhelm III during the post-Napoleonic era when there was a great burst of creative expansion in both Potsdam and Berlin. As in the urns shown previously the micro-mosaics reflect a fascination in Antique discoveries in Italy.

An English adaptation of this neo-classical vase shape is seen in a garniture of three Spode vases (fig. 354). With gilded handles and painted on both sides with bouquets of spring and summer flowers on a dark blue ground richly decorated with gilding in a scale design, these are marked 'Spode' and with the design number 1166. They date from about 1820. The larger vase is 12 in. high. A smaller but charming piece of English porcelain of slightly earlier (circa 1800) is an inkstand from the Worcester factory of Flight, Barr and Barr (fig. 355). The orange ground is gilded with foliate

354

A fine garniture of three Spode vases of about 1820, splendidly painted with spring and summer flowers.

patterns and a main panel is painted with feathers. The inkstand has three pots and a swan neck handle. It is 6¾ in. long.

Very unusual and decorative are sets of painted tôle birds and fungi that were made in France in around 1850 (figs 356 and 357). We have seen two sets of each. Life size, the birds and fungi are in the form of tôle plaques

355

A Worcester factory Flight, Barr and Barr porcelain inkstand with an orange ground and painted with feathers.

356

A very rare collection of life size tôle bird plaques on weighted stands, made in France in about 1850.

357

Part of a collection of tôle painted mushrooms and fungi standing on weighted bases. French, circa 1850.

358
A small collection of
late nineteenth
century turned and
carved ivory frames.

fixed to weighted bases and in each case they represent real species. The birds, all native varieties, include mallard, teal, lapwing, goldfinch, firecrest, yellowhammer, crossbill, blackcap, nuthatch and tree creeper. The tôle mushrooms and toadstools, of which there are twenty-eight in all (fewer shown here), again demonstrate true specimens. It is believed that these may have been made for an apothecary whose duty it was to be able to identify the varieties with regard to their edibility or danger. The fungi are mostly known in Britain, though Caesar's mushroom for example is a Mediterranean species. The English names are enough to stimulate hallucinogenic poetry: Slimy Milk Cap, Blue-Yellow Russula, Horn of Plenty, Fly Agaric, Stinking Parasol, Livid Entoloma, Amethyst Deceiver, The Prince, Rose Gilled Grisette, The Panther, etc.

One of the delights of being at the centre of a colonial empire was having opportunities of importing from distant countries fine materials for craftsmanship. Mahogany was the most important of these. On a lesser but still notable scale was ivory. Though we now hate the thought of killing elephants it has to be remembered that hunting them was once a very different matter, when there were great quantities of self sustaining herds in plenty of space in natural habitats. It is the shortage of habitat that makes it essential for us now to preserve the sadly reduced numbers of wild animals. We can continue to treasure ivory objects made in the past. They are very beautiful. A small collection of ivory photograph frames is shown in fig. 358. Made around the turn of the nineteenth and twentieth centuries each of these is turned and carved to make attractive use of this wonderful material.

More birds are depicted in a group of Swiss cast brass birds of about 1880 (fig. 359). Partridges, curlew, snipe and kookaburra are realistically modelled, sculpted and painted, simply as objects in the much loved tradition of admiring the species of wildlife that was a paramount interest in Victorian England, and in Europe generally.

Gathered together on the top of a Sheraton satinwood pembroke table is a collection of ladies' bibelots, mostly for their dressing tables (fig. 360).

360
On a lady's dressing
table is a large
Palais Royal mother
of pearl mirror and a
number of later
nineteenth century
objects including
ivory ring stands.

359
A group of Swiss
cast brass and
pained birds, all
native to England
except for a
kookaburra.

361
*A pair of large
decalcomania glass
vases, the print and
coloured decoration
being applied to the
inside. French,
circa 1840.*

362
*A splendid pair of
large Bohemian
opaline vases of
about 1845.*

A very large and splendid Palais Royal mirror is veneered with mother of pearl with gilt ormolu mounts as in the smaller pieces shown above on page 269. A single cut glass candlestick with drops, of about 1840, contains a sulphide portrait of the young Queen Victoria and next to that are three carved ivory ring stands made for a Bond Street shop early in this (twentieth) century. The other objects include a pair of purple glass hyacinth vases with gilt decoration, three cut glass scent bottles (again featuring sulphide miniatures), a tortoiseshell brush and mirror with gold piqué decoration, a tortoiseshell and silver ink stand, and a diamanté photograph frame with paste 'stones' and a red glass border. All of these date from the end of the nineteenth century and were made in England.

This eclectic anthology of special objects ends with two pairs of large sized glass or semi-glass vases. The first is a pair of French decalcomania cylindrical beaker shaped vases, 17¾ in. high (fig. 344). Made in about 1840 and undoubtedly inspired originally by Chinese porcelain, decalcomania is a technique of découpage where coloured transfers or cut-out prints are applied to the reverse of glass and then decorated over the back with a colour, in this case white. The subjects frequently have a chinoiserie flavour with humorous fantasy derived from the Regency extravagances made famous at the Brighton Pavilion.

Lastly is a magnificent pair of Bohemian opaline vases of circa 1845 (fig. 362). These splendid baroque shaped urns of semi translucent 'glass porcelain' opaline stand 18½ in. tall and are decorated with effulgent flowers and fruit on a soft cigar-brown ground, while contrasting areas are decorated with gilded ornament on the basic white material.

363

One last object: this mid-eighteenth century Venetian crib of gondola form is carved, painted and gilded with typical rococo decoration and with circular cartouches showing gilt putti on a blue ground.

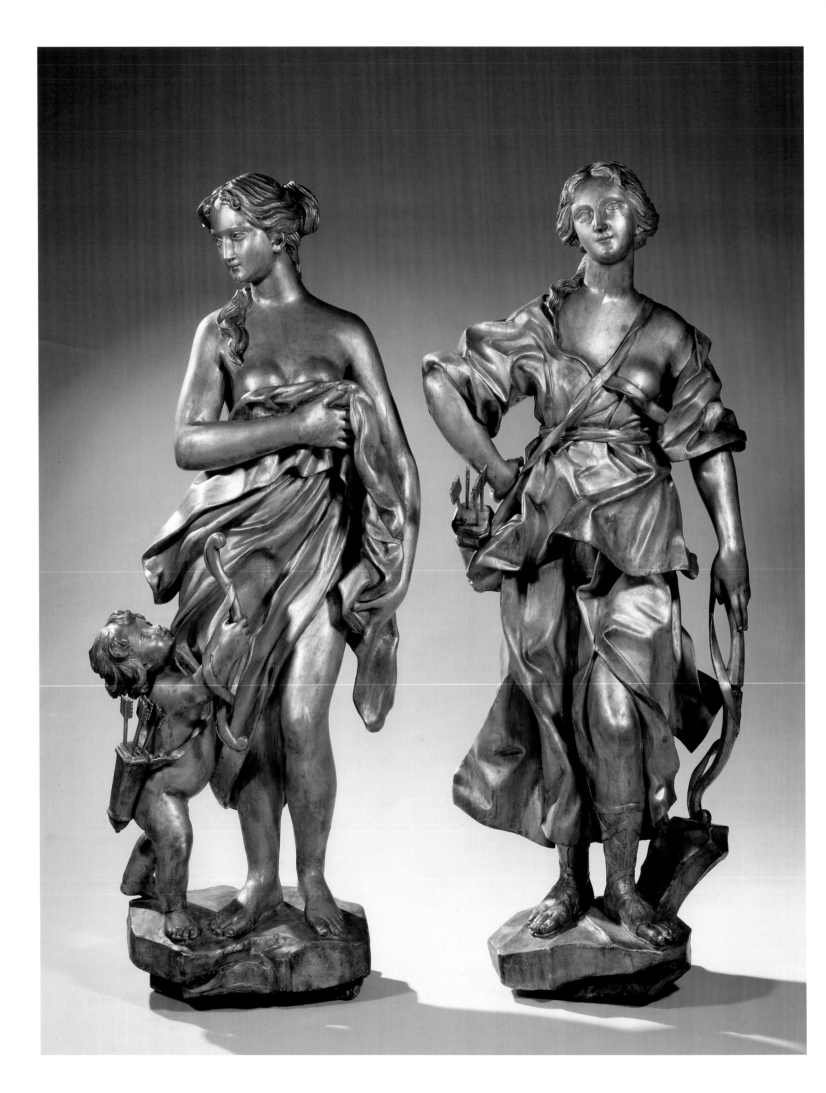

Anecdote and Character

——————◆——————

I NEVITABLY, we are lucky enough at Mallett's to be meeting interesting people all the time, and people interested in our chosen field. There used to be a pattern to their visits, and clients could be expected at specific times in the year. It was indeed often seasonal and Francis Egerton, in his day, expected certain visitors at regular intervals. On one occasion however, a grande dame who always came to Mallett's in November appeared somewhat earlier. When remarked upon she explained that this year she just could not wait for the leaves to fall and had her gardeners pick the leaves off the trees. Francis Egerton probably liked this, as he himself had something of a leaf fetish. He would rake the gravel in his garden twice a day to remove untidy leaves. More than that he would hose down the laid stones and gravel, as he preferred the darker and shiny look!

On another occasion Peter Maitland looked after two sisters. They also came regularly each year to see 'dear Mr Nickerson' and always bought something. This time however David was away and so Peter greeted them at Bourdon House. They were short, fat and determined. One wore a full-length mink coat and the other Persian lamb, both with matching hats. 'Mink' wanted a bureau plat (pronounced like flat) and was shown one downstairs, in kingwood with ormolu mounts. She wanted it. 'Persian lamb' said she wanted one too and was told of another upstairs, in ebonised kingwood, with ormolu mounts, about the same price. As 'Persian lamb' climbed very slowly up the creaking stairs in Bourdon House, 'Mink' said to her 'Be careful how you go sister, mind the banisters'. She then turned to Peter and said 'I said that because if my sister sees something she wants she goes in a straight line for it, whether there are banisters there or not!'

Peter also tells a story of another lady, who was a regular visitor and the bored wife of an American ambassador. She swanned into the Bond Street shop, swinging her hips very slowly, trying to look incredibly sexy, and said, 'I have just spent two hours with your lovely Mr Yorke, now it's your turn'. She was one of the biggest time wasters of all time, took hundreds

364
A pair of three-quarter life size South German carved wood figures, representing Venus and Diana and retaining their original gilding. Circa 1750.

365

A finely carved pair of large ivory candelabra with leaf, tulip and magnolia motifs, signed 'Flli Coselschi Fecero nell'Anno 1897'.

366

This large and intricately turned ivory cup (28½ in. tall) was made on a Holtzapffel lathe, an 'engine of civilisation' for amateur recreation. Circa 1870.

of photographs and details and also used her own camera, one-handed, trying to look casual. It was stiflingly hot outside and when she had done the rounds of the ground floor rooms she said she wanted to go downstairs. Peter's heart sank. He said truthfully, that there was no air-conditioning downstairs and was she sure she wanted to face the heat. She slowly swivelled around on one leg and gave him a penetrating, sensuous look and said, measuredly, 'I promise you I never wilt'.

Which reminds me of a reported client, of many years back; I will call her Mrs Miriam C. Black. An immaculately turned out American lady (they were always well dressed) came in grandly, followed by a rather small husband. She said, 'my name is Mrs Miriam C. Black, wife of Ambassador Black, who is behind'.

It may have been the same lady, or perhaps another, who on arrival was heard to say 'Clear the shop'. But many others were more restrained and dignified. A much-loved and incredibly rich wife with her charming old world husband used to visit us very regularly. She was a woman of few words however. When she arrived one day she came in and saw the most expensive piece of furniture Mallett had ever had. She gave one glance at it and said she wanted to go to the john. When she came back her husband said 'Do you like this piece?' She nodded. 'Do you want it?' he drawled. She replied 'Ugh, hgh'.

The majority of our clients are delightful and share our enthusiasms. They have an interest in beautiful things, and in fine furniture and love it. On the whole furniture lacks vulgarity or conspicuous ostentation. Naturally a few who seem to live on a more showy plane come and look at our things but don't usually buy from us. I was taking a friendly Middle Eastern lady around one day who was apparently laden with money. We found ourselves talking about this and that. She told me she had had her handbag stolen in Harrods and had lost a lot of money. She said her husband wasn't pleased. There was a pause and she confessed a little conspiratorially: 'But I didn't tell him about the jewel'. It was clear that that was a much more serious matter.

No two reactions to our extensive collection of furniture and works of art are the same and some are prepared to share their views more than others. Some express great joy in seeing wonderful things while others more conspiratorially apparently discover treasures hidden amongst our stock that we perhaps hadn't noticed. Best of all is sharing the beauty of the lovely things that we have to offer. One of the most touching incidents that I heard of only recently was of a blind man who would come in to buy pictures, his wife and our people describing them to him in detail. I love to think of the spiritual sensation, an experience beyond the physical, that the blind person practised in considering art in this way.

367
An unusual George II pedestal desk of oak oyster-veneered with olivewood, patinated by age to a wonderful colour.

Miscellaneous Treasures

BEING a specialist collector in one chosen field can provide a totally absorbing interest that opens up even deeper fascination. My own private passion happens to be seventeenth and eighteenth century needlework. In pursuing more and more knowledge and experience in this relatively small field I have discovered that I shall never master it totally, though I may accumulate more knowledge than most others about it and derive enormous satisfaction from an in-depth involvement in this field.

But when it comes to living in the real world I would argue equally strongly that an eclectic interest in as wide a range as possible brings about a happy and contented mind. In terms of collecting and furnishing one's 'castle' Englishmen have a reputation for broad ranging tastes. Carefully selected variety is the spice of life. The following selection of miscellaneous pieces further reflects Mallett's wide ranging business in dealing in things of all sorts that have quality and charm. The first picture (fig. 368) shows a very fine marble chimney piece of the first half of the eighteenth century, together with an Adam period polished steel grate and a fine contemporary fender of paktong, a non-tarnishing alloy of copper, zinc and nickel derived from Chinese coinage, and a pair of Louis XVI fire dogs. There is an unusually large English eighteenth century needlework picture above of elegant ladies in a landscape gathering the fruits of the earth.

My next two selections are of further age-old marbles, both wonderful stone specimens. Fig. 369 shows a magnificent late seventeenth century wine cooler of Rouge Royale de Gochenée marble. It is a beautiful example of the kind of basin that was a familiar feature of Louis XIV buffets where plate would be displayed and wine served as well as glasses washed and filled.

Fig. 370 shows one of a pair of specimen marble table tops, which were formerly at Kimbolton Castle, Huntingdonshire. These are fine examples of colourful marble tops made in Italy for visiting English gentry who travelled there as young men doing the Grand Tour, in a combined expedition of

368

A fine English fireplace of Carrara marble carved in the classical manner, complete with an Adam steel grate and a paktong fender.

369

*A magnificent
seventeenth century
French marble
wine cooler.*

370

*One of a pair of
marble tops,
5 ft 9 in. long, this
and its companion
piece consists of an
extensive collection
of interesting stones
brought home from
Italy as a souvenir of
the Grand Tour.*

scholarly education and amusement. Such marbles would be sent home, to be made up as tables with bases of various kinds. This pair are each 5 ft 9 in. by 2 ft 9 in. and include rare stones.

Of the early eighteenth century is a charming walnut spinet on its original stand (fig. 371). This keyboard instrument has five octaves, the keys being of ebony with white incidentals and behind the keyboard is a marquetry panel. The word spinet is derived from the Italian spinetta, diminutive of spina, a thorn, for the plucking quills of the mechanism are like thorns. 'Bentside' spinets, such as this, were popular in England as they were small, easier to maintain than harpsichords and yet produced a powerful tone. They had one set of strings, plucked by crow quills. The simple turned stand is elegant and practical. The stool with it is of walnut, also of about 1710 and upholstered with contemporary needlework.

From far afield is a series of Indian pieces commissioned by Europeans living and working there in the pursuit of colonial business or military

371

A charming early eighteenth century walnut spinet on its original stand, with a contemporary stool.

protection. Two outstanding bureau bookcases (figs 372 and 373), were made in Vizagapatam in around 1740, conforming to familiar English shapes but decorated with ivory inlay of entirely Indian form. As with textile patterns, the combination of Anglo-Indian features is extremely fortuitous, and indeed the ivory decoration of these pieces owes much to textile designs. The two cabinets vary slightly, one having ebony mouldings at the top and base, and each has differences in the ivory inlay. The smaller bookcase (fig. 373) has tortoiseshell fronted drawers in the interior. Also extremely rare, and from the same workshops, north of Madras, is a pair of ivory inlaid armchairs (fig. 374), again of teak with engraved ivory marquetry. The technique of ivory inlay was practised in several parts of India for European merchants but it had originally been developed for Moghul rulers and through Jesuit missionaries for local use as well as for export. The designs were firstly imitating European ivory and metalwork patterns as familiar on armoury, especially the stocks of guns, but Moghul flower and plant forms were soon expanded and became even more suitable for larger areas on boxes and cabinet furniture. Gradually these softened into even larger continuous patterns, as on these chairs and the two bureau bookcases above. Also Indian and of ivory is a splendid armchair (fig. 375) but unlike the Vizagapatam furniture this has more of a Portuguese and native Indian feel. In this case the wooden chair frame is entirely covered

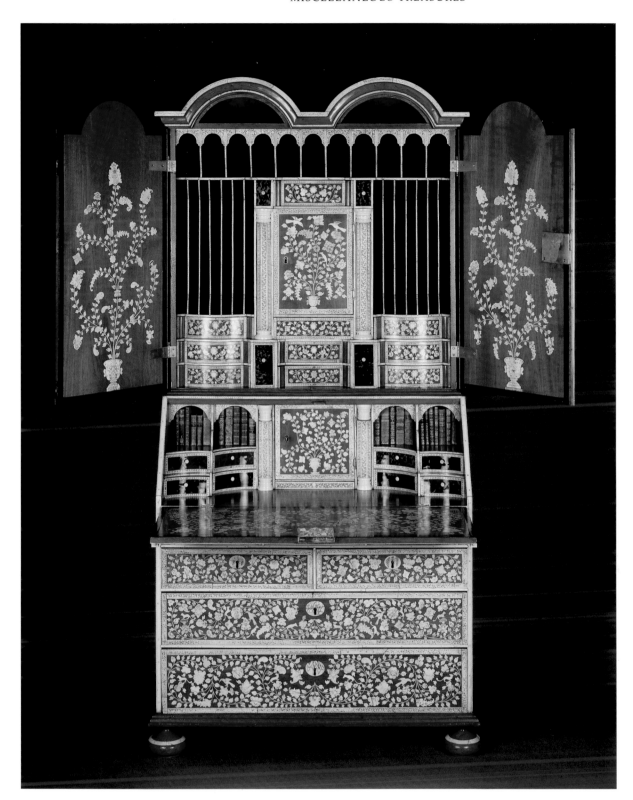

373
*Another remarkable
Indian bureau
bookcase of English
form inlaid with
ivory in patterns
derived from
textiles.
Circa 1740.*

372
*An extraordinary
Indian bureau
bookcase made for
a European with
elaborate ivory
marquetry set into
teak and with ebony
mouldings at top
and bottom.*

with pieces of ivory pinned on with nails and it has delicate engraved decoration. Solid ivory Hindu deity bird and monkey masks form terminals on the armrests and on the front seat rail. The chair dates from the mid-nineteenth century.

Returning to England, we have an apparently mundane object but in fact an extraordinarily luxurious spinning wheel (fig. 376). This delightful working object is made of the finest mahogany with ivory fittings including labels indicating that it was supplied by John Hardy, who continued a

374

A very rare pair of armchairs which like the previously illustrated cabinets were made at Vizagapatam in about 1740.

375

A mid-nineteenth century Indian armchair entirely veneered with pieces of ivory and with decorative etching and nailing.

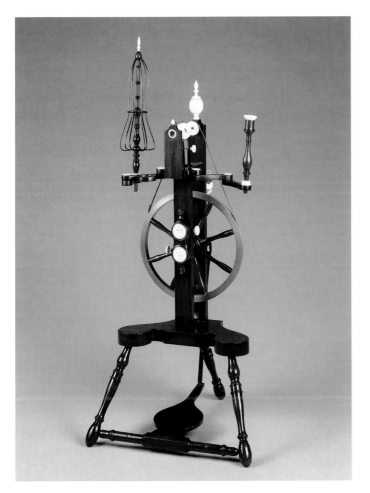

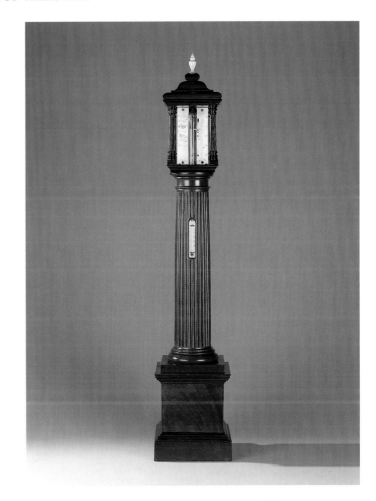

376

An exceptional spinning wheel of mahogany with ivory fittings suited to gracious arcadian activity. Circa 1825.

377

A massive mahogany stick barometer in the form of a lighthouse. Circa 1830.

business started by Doughty in York. Clearly made for a privileged lady, this fits into the much loved arcadian theme of participation in rural activities, and can be dated to about 1825. Almost certainly made for a man on the other hand, is another glorious toy, an impressive and rare mahogany barometer of about 1830 (fig. 377). This massive stick barometer stands 3 ft 6 in. tall and is in the form of a miniature lighthouse. The silvered dial is signed 'E. Dawes Whitehaven' while the ivory thermometer on the front of the fluted column is by D. Davis, London.

Fig. 380 illustrates a rare and beautiful Irish marble fireplace in the scagliola technique associated with Pietro Bossi, an Italian craftsman who worked in Dublin between 1785 and 1798. Coloured composition is inlaid in neo-classical arabesque forms with leaf motifs, paterae, and ribbon-tied garlands of ivy leaves. The fireplace still has its original engraved brass register grate and fender, all Irish of the late eighteenth century, and from Rossmore House, Monaghan, Ireland.

Also from Ireland is an embossed paper picture in its original japanned frame (fig. 378). Of about 1760 this is by Samuel Dixon who was famed for several series of such pictures depicting flowers, birds or a combination of both as in this case. The pictures often retain original labels on the back with charming lengthy dedications to noble patrons and with accounts of the origin of the more exotic birds that are sometimes depicted. Here we have a homely goldfinch, familiar flowers and a fictitious butterfly, painted in gouache and each form raised by embossing from behind.

378

An embossed paper
gouache painting by
Samuel Dixon of
Dublin in its
original chinoiserie
frame.

A wonderful pair of horn shaped vases, rhytons, are shown in fig. 379. These were just one item in a service of Paris porcelain signed by Pierre Neppel who was famed for innovative techniques including a masterful use of gilt transfer and relief decoration.

Natural wonders are of course far greater than anything man can create but when man presents them artistically indoors they can have great effect and celebrate creation not normally seen. A handsome entomological cabinet made by T. Gurney in about 1905 (fig. 381) contains fifty-six collecting drawers for specimens and about 1600 butterflies from many

379

A splendid pair of
gilt porcelain
rhytons, classical
drinking horns, as
ornamental vases,
signed by Pierre
Neppel, Paris,
circa 1815.

380

This Irish scagliola
fireplace in a
technique perfected
by Pietro Bossi
retains its original
engraved brass
register grate and
fender. Circa 1790.

381

*Preserved in a
cabinet of the early
twentieth century
are 56 drawers of
butterflies from
many parts of
the world.*

382

*One of a pair of
cabinets containing
a collection of
stuffed birds from
Australia and
South America,
dated 1834.*

383

This pair of massive throne chairs were made by a pupil of John Makepeace in the 1970s. They are of Californian myrtle.

parts of the world, all safely preserved and shut away from destructive light – away from the sunshine that gives their species life. Collections such as these must be regarded as scientific studies which bring about true appreciation and a desire to learn about nature. In 1834 a collector assembled a variety of beautiful birds from Australia and South America in two cabinets. Fig. 382 shows one of these. A wonderful mixture of birds is displayed in settings with branches behind glass.

A last phenomenon of Nature, helped by artistic inspiration and for use indoors is a pair of huge throne-like chairs of Californian myrtle (fig. 383). These were made about twenty years ago by a pupil of John Makepeace, Nick Moverly, from the complete bowl of a tree trunk and in such a manner that they can be used either way up, revealing the polished inside burr grain or an outward flowing cope-like surface of the knotty wood. This interesting modern furniture celebrates with sensitive craftsmanship the innate wonder of the most important element, the beautiful wood. I hope that in many years to come these will be enjoyed alongside the spectacular triumphs of proportion, design and workmanship of the great furniture of Georgian England. In all antique furniture we can sense a live, creative and natural beauty.

> *'Things men have made with wakened hand, and put soft life into, are awake through years with transferred touch, and go on glowing for long years. And for this reason, some old things are lovely, warm still with the life of forgotten men who made them.'*
>
> D. H. Lawrence

Sculpture

⸺◆⸺

SINCE so much of the history of the decorative arts stems from Louis XIV's ambitious works at Versailles and the Sun King's influence on other aspiring European royal courts, it is appropriate perhaps to begin an interlude on sculpture with a famous bronze of that king. Fig. 384 shows a smaller version of a colossal equestrian statue of Louis XIV by François Girardon that was destroyed in 1792. This reduced model, following ones of similar scale made under Girardon's supervision, is finely cast and patinated. It stands on an ebony veneered pedestal inlaid with borders of brass in *contre-partie*, and with ormolu mouldings and mounts including an elaborate figure of Time. This sculpture was formerly in the collection of Sir Philip Sassoon Bt, and latterly at Houghton Hall, Norfolk.

Of the Louis XV period are a superb pair of terracotta animals, a sheep and a goat (figs 386 and 387). Made to life size, these rare and charming figures represent the height of rococo delight in out of doors life, of arcadian pleasures and especially the tending of sheep and milking cows, themes often expressed in needlework and porcelain. These two animals are said to have come from the Chateau de Bellevue, near Versailles, which was built for Madame de Pompadour, the favourite of Louis XV. The sheep and the goat are each seated calmly, one foot forward, the sheep with a fleecy coat, while the distinctively hairy goat is partially garlanded and nibbling Bacchanalian grapes.

Bacchus himself is the subject of the next illustration (fig. 388), a superb lead model of the god by John Cheere, of about 1740. Six feet high, the figure is crowned with a wreath of grapes and vine leaves and holds up a goblet. Standing in the classical *contrapposto* manner, he is clothed in a wolf's pelt and retains some of the original paint work. When originally supplied, lead figures were painted in bright and naturalistic colours, though we have now grown to like them in a weathered state. Bacchus (the Roman counterpart of Dionysus) is of pagan origin. He was the god of wine and revelry and a

384
A fine nineteenth century version of a colossal bronze statue of Louis XIV by Girardon that used to stand in what is now the Place Vendôme in Paris.

365
Louis XIV, after Girardon.

favourite emblem in gardens and dining rooms. John Cheere was a prolific maker of lead figures, working at Hyde Park corner, having taken over the Van Nost family workshop. His brother, Sir Henry Cheere was famed for marble sculpture but John turned to the more commercial and varied business of casting figures in lead.

A very rare and beautiful carved marble stool, in neo-classical form, (fig. 391) is ascribed to a design by Charles Tatham. Of breche violette marble, the rectangular stool is carved with swagged drapery on all sides and with a fringe around the edge, the stool legs being deeply fluted and headed by rosettes. Probably made in England, or possibly France, in about 1810, this object epitomises the 'noble simplicity and calm grandeur' fashionable amongst aesthetes at this time, especially for neo-classical entrance halls which would impress with such an atmosphere in preparation for the sumptuous rooms beyond. Tatham was an architect who travelled extensively and advised Henry Holland who worked for the Prince Regent at Carlton House.

386 and 387
*Life size terracotta sculptures of a sheep and
a Bacchanalian goat. French, circa 1760.*

389

*Almost unnervingly
lifelike is a cold
painted terracotta
sculpture of an owl.
French or possibly
Austrian,
circa 1880.*

390

*Romantic or
sentimental, in the
mid-nineteenth
century there was
widespread interest
in wildlife and a
passion for animal
and bird sculpture.
This Viennese eagle
in limewood was
made in about 1860.*

From austere classicism we move to later nineteenth century realism and naturalistic sculptures. The first two are from Nature itself and the last is that most famous of all emblems of the last century, Queen Victoria. Fig. 389 shows a late nineteenth century large-scale model of an owl in terracotta, painted in a lifelike manner, perched on a branch. Mallett's have seen three almost identical versions of this sculpture, which were made in France or possibly Austria. The overall height of the piece is 24¾ inches.

Another bird, of a similar scale, is an eagle carved in wood (fig. 390). This noble creature is certainly Viennese. He is carved in limewood, then singed

388

*A splendid lead
statue of Bacchus,
the Roman god of
wine and revelry,
by John Cheere,
circa 1740.*

391

*The epitome of neo-
classical decoration,
this early nineteenth
century marble stool
is attributed to
Charles Tatham.
It represents the
combination of
'noble simplicity and
calm grandeur'.*

392
*This life-sized
terracotta sculpture
of the young
Queen Victoria
was made in
Edinburgh and
is an extraordinary
feat of pottery.*

to achieve dark markings, stained and wax polished to a pleasing effect. This
was a time when naturalism was highly respected, and the wildlife of the
highlands was especially valued, as typified by the works of Sir Walter Scott
and also by Queen Victoria's passion for her Scottish home, Balmoral Castle.

Magnificent terracotta sculptures (figs 392 and 393) of the young Queen
Victoria and Prince Albert, the Prince Consort stand 6 ft 6 in. high. Prince
Albert's statue is stamped on the plinth 'John Millar, Potter to Her Majesty
Edinburgh', and 'Grangemouth Terracotta Works'. The Queen is shown in

393
Prince Albert is shown holding a scroll perhaps referring to a plan or a doctorate.

ermine edged robes, and bearing the orb of state, while Prince Albert is in military uniform and carrying a scroll. Both wear insignia of the Order of the Garter. These extraordinarily large feats of pottery were apparently made possible by being sent for firing to industrial kilns at Grangemouth on the Firth of Forth, not far from Edinburgh, an ingenious solution to the difficult task of creating such large sculptures. It is fitting that these two figures have returned to Edinburgh, to stand in perpetuity in the National Museum of Scotland.

394

A particularly elegant Carlton House writing
table attributed to John McLean, of rosewood
with gilt metal mounts and giltwood
mouldings.

The Regency Period

―――――――――

THE Prince of Wales was Regent from 1811 to 1820 when he acceded to the throne as George IV but the term Regency in relation to the decorative arts is usually applied to the first quarter of the nineteenth century. The prevalent styles during this time developed out of the neat and tidy neo-classical taste of the previous century and alongside the development of Empire fashions in France as they followed on from the Louis XVI period.

Early Regency furniture has much of the elegant simplicity of line that is associated with Thomas Sheraton whose influential *Cabinet Maker's and Upholsterer's Drawing-Book* was published in 1793 reflecting patterns already established amongst the leading furniture makers. Gradually, more sumptuous details were added, however, at first in terms of smaller ornament and then developing into more dramatically sculptural shapes for the whole piece.

Two beautiful Carlton House writing tables suggest by their name a central influence of their time, that of the Prince Regent whose passion for interior decoration was unbounded and exciting. Carlton House was his first great project and the Brighton Pavilion his most theatrical. The first Carlton House desk (fig. 394) is of faded rosewood and perhaps made by John McLean. It is typical of the form that is given this popular name. Some are of plainer mahogany but this is elegantly and smartly dressed with polished brass and gilt reeded mouldings, brass beaded mouldings around the drawer fronts, gilt rings round the turned legs and a pierced brass gallery around the back of the superstructure. All these are familiar features of the period, adding a certain showiness. Also of rosewood, the second writing table (fig. 395), which is said to have been one of a pair made for Lord Sandwich, is even more demonstrably Regency in a few aspects. The strictly geometrical half round shape is a notable feature of early nineteenth century design, but the neat cabinetmaking is thoroughly eighteenth century. However, the Pharaoh masks are derived from ornament in Empire

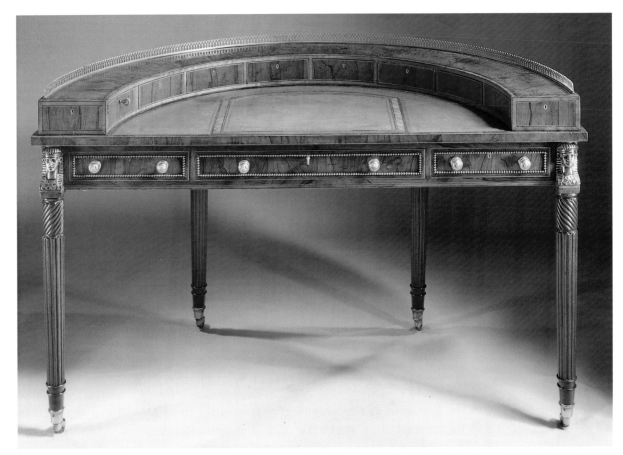

395
Another Regency writing table of semicircular shape with the Empire feature of Pharoah head masks. Circa 1810.

396
An elegant pair of globes, celestial and terrestrial, on mahogany tripod stands with compasses. Circa 1800.

397
*Even small pieces of
occasional furniture
could be made
with remarkable
originality and
with extraordinary
attention to detail.
Circa 1810.*

furniture inspired by Napoleon's Egyptian campaign. In addition the spiral turned, and reverse fluted or thickly reeded legs are features that gradually became more prominent in the nineteenth century (cf. also fig. 440).

A lovely pair of standing globes (fig. 396), have all the elegance of the early Regency. With maker's labels and dated (unfortunately not recorded but perhaps by Carey and circa 1800), they stand on downward curling tripod legs with stretchers holding compasses. One globe shows the Earth,

398
*A smart and elegant
coromandel wood
sofa table of about
1810 has double
column end
supports, a double
stretcher, and stands
on downward
curving legs, all
variants on earlier
varieties of this
type of table.*

399
A charming pair of Dutch pewter chestnut urns with red and gold decoration and painted scenes resembling drawings. Circa 1800.

the other shows the heavens. The mahogany stems have turned vases in the centre.

Satinwood was still fashionable, especially the more richly marked varieties as shown in an unusual and beautifully detailed étagère of about 1810 (fig. 397). Contrasting plain golden surfaces with crisply ornamented detailing this has Grecian turned side supports with gilded tulip-like mouldings and is further enriched with metalwork, a pierced brass gallery, a brass grill lined with silk, edge mouldings on the side panels and vertical swags of husks on the front. The Regency period is characterised generally by stronger forms, stronger colours and bolder woods. Fig. 398 shows a splendid sofa table, of classic form but with many new aspects, most noticeably the bold colouring of the coromandel or calamander wood from India. This strongly marked veneer is relieved by satinwood crossbanding framing the top and numerous small gilt metal mounts. The supports are of double columns joined by double turned stretchers, with a central plinth, and standing on downward curving legs.

Another example of the much-favoured rosewood is seen in a neat Regency standing bookcase which is double sided (fig. 400). This has a marble top and a pierced brass gallery. The corners are in the form of external columns with brass filled fluting, resting on the four legs. Also from the library is a handsome pair of armchairs of mahogany and with caned seats, backs and sides and nice old leather cushions (fig. 401). Their elegant form is neo-classical, based on the depiction of Greek chairs in sculptural reliefs, with 'sabre' curved front legs, back legs and arm supports. Having completed the Grand Tour, gentlemen liked to furnish their houses with antique souvenirs from their travels and modern furniture that emulated the noble styles of the ancients.

I showed examples of painted tôle earlier (see page 268). This included a pair of chestnut urns. I now illustrate a similar pair, but this time of pewter, and made in Holland and painted with Dutch scenes. Urns such as these are said to have been made in England if they are of tin (tôle) and Holland if

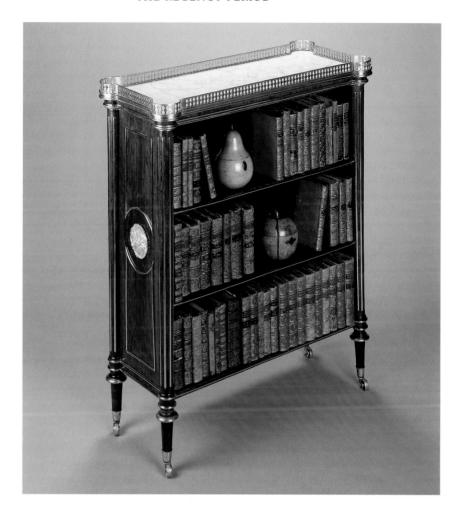

401
The design inspired by 'antique' chairs depicted in ancient sculpture and vase painting, these Regency chairs are elegant, comfortable and timeless.

400
A small Regency bookcase on castors is of rosewood with a marble top and brass gallery and has shelves on both sides.

402
A splendid Regency harp with red 'japanned' decoration that includes Prince of Wales feathers amongst its neo-Grecian ornament.

403
Austere in form this round table of coromandel wood on a tripod base represents the later Grecian variety of neo-classicism.

404

A magnificent Regency occasional table richly decorated but chiefly displaying a fine collection of semi precious marbles in the top.

they are of pewter. This pair (fig. 399) is particularly beautiful, of an elegant shape and finely decorated in red and gold with the Dutch vignettes. There is also room for another harp. This one (fig. 402) is a fine one of about 1810 made by Schwieso, Grosjean and Co., of Soho Square, London. The pillar is decorated with carved gesso caryatids and a frieze of musical muses in bright burnished and matt gilding. The soundboard retains its original gilt decoration on a red ground, including Prince of Wales feathers.

405

An octagonal carved rosewood centre table of about 1840, the top with fine pietra dura *panels in the seventeenth century manner.*

406

One of a pair of Empire ormolu wall lights is in an attractive light design of hunting horns hung from an inverted arrow.

407

Greek, Egyptian and Etruscan elements were united with Roman antiquity in later Regency and Empire decorative arts. The language of such motifs has an original and distinctive character epitomised by these tôle lamps.

Three very good Regency tables each have special qualities of the period. The first is a round centre table of calamander wood supported on a tripod base with three carved giltwood paw feet (fig. 403). Deliberately austere, the top is banded with the same wood, the figuring running in contrasting directions. The second is a smaller occasional table (fig. 404) of wonderful quality and very rich in design with a combination of marbles, brass inlay in the rosewood surfaces, brass mouldings and carved giltwood. Very much of the Prince Regent's taste, this is primarily a magnificent vehicle for the top, a splendid collection of semi precious stones. A drawer in the frieze contains a panel with a key to each of the one hundred and twenty varieties. Brass inlay, as on this small table, was another much favoured form of Regency decoration, usually in rosewood, that became increasingly popular through the century. The boulle technique of brass and tortoiseshell marquetry also enjoyed a revival (see pages 332 and 333), and eventually dominated a great body of poor quality Victorian furniture. Of very distinguished quality however, this table is in the manner of George Bullock, cabinetmaker, restorer and dealer who specialised in fine brass and tortoiseshell inlaid furniture, as did Thomas Parker and Louis le Gaigneur. The third Regency table is a small octagonal centre table of veneered and solid rosewood (fig. 405), finely carved with strong motifs. The top is again of precious

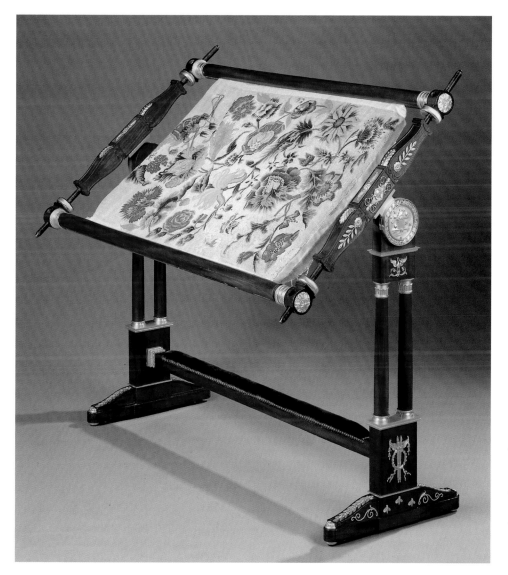

408
A rich and unusual piece of Napoleonic furniture attributed to Jacob is a mahogany sewing frame of about 1800 with numerous familiar motifs in the ormolu mounts, including bees on the feet.

409
*A magnificent
English mahogany
wine cooler of
sarcophagus shape,
the woodwork of
exceptional colour,
with bronze
patinated mounts
including a seated
lion on the top.
Circa 1820.*

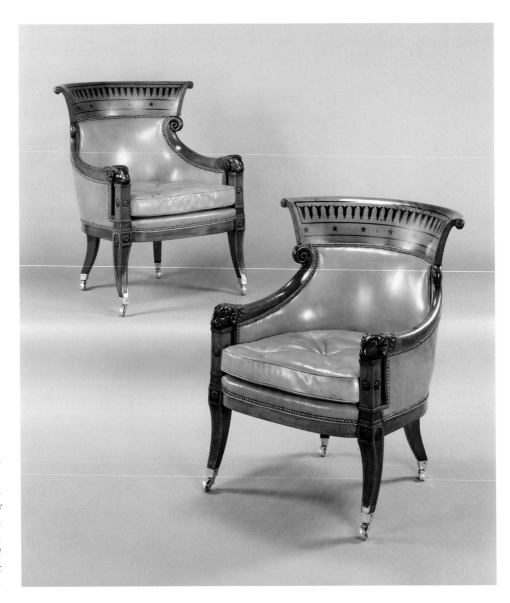

410
*The ebony inlay on
these magnificent
Regency chairs of
Grecian form is
inspired by Etruscan
decoration and
painting on Greek
vases. Circa 1815.*

411

A fine pair of Regency mahogany chairs with Royal Arms made for official use in the former colony of British Guyana.

marbles, this time *pietra dura* pictures in the seventeenth century manner with birds on branches inset into panels. Of about 1840, the table is attributed to the furniture makers Banting, France and Co.

Aspects of the French Empire style are seen in three more items. A pair of ormolu wall lights (fig. 406) are in light neo-classical form, four horns pinned to an arrow by a lion mask, while above that there is a sun disc with Apollo's mask and a palmette tail to the arrow. A pair of painted tôle oil lamps (fig. 407) are in the form of miniature Greek columns on plinths supported by classical paw and leaf brackets. They have engraved and frosted glass dome shades standing on elaborately pierced rims. These are French, circa 1820. Much richer, is a magnificent Empire adjustable frame for needlework of about 1800 (fig. 408), of mahogany with Napoleonic ormolu mounts including a relief patera of a beehive on the hinge and further bees on the feet. In the manner of François-Honoré Georges Jacob, this piece is related in design to commissions from the Jacob firm for the Grand Trianon at Versailles and the Palais des Tuileries.

A magnificent English sarcophagus-shaped wine cooler of circa 1820 (fig. 409), is of mahogany of superb figuring and colour. The top hinges open to reveal its original lead lining and a plug hole allowing it to be drained. On the lid a bronze lion sits within a carved palisade while lion mask ring handles and rose paterae decorate the corners and sides of this splendid dining room piece. Also of mahogany is an interesting pair of large Regency armchairs made for the use of the Royal Family in British Guyana (fig. 411), which gained independence in 1966. Two chairs en suite are now in the National Museum of Guyana and related patterns are in the Victoria and Albert Museum and the Metropolitan Museum, New York. The chairs are boldly carved with a number of Greek neo-classical motifs and have the Royal Arms painted in circular panels in the backs.

412

Inspired by Greek painted vases and Etruscan wall painting, another aspect of Regency furniture is mahogany with ebony marquetry, mouldings and carved ornament. A pair of tub-shaped chairs reflect this (fig. 410). Deep coved back rails show this Greek or Etruscan mood while downward scrolling arms end in ram's heads above sabre legs. The chairs are of a form associated with Thomas Hope whose personal collection and designs for his own house were of this hybrid classical style, and became influential.

One of the most ubiquitous expressions of Empire and Regency neo-classical furniture was the chaise longue, a day-bed for the drawing room in Greek or Roman form. There were many variations but one of my favourites is illustrated in fig. 412. This boat-like sofa stands on animal legs reminiscent of a crocodile, just one of several creatures that percolated into furniture design following Napoleon's Egyptian campaign. The front end is shell shaped while the other is more traditional. The piece is japanned in black and gold with a mask of Athena within a laurel wreath on the inside. This is probably English rather than French and made in about 1815.

The most famous naval victory of all time was probably the battle of Trafalgar when Admiral Lord Nelson established British supremacy in 1805 and died on board his flagship, H.M.S. *Victory*. A fascinating carved chair,

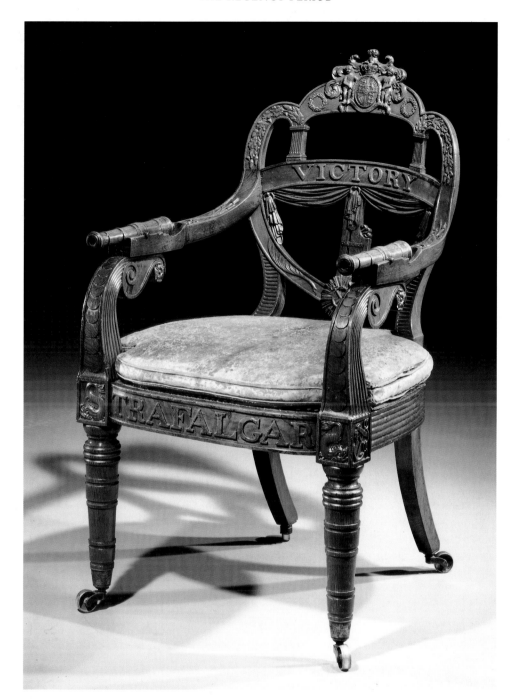

413

This fascinating 'Victory' chair was made in commemoration of the Battle of Trafalgar using oak removed from H.M.S. Victory, *Nelson's flagship, in 1806.*

stamped *L. Abington Sculptorit* was made from oak taken from the ship and is thought to have been made for the Prime Minister, William Pitt the younger (fig. 413). Pitt died in 1806 however, and it was presented to his elder brother, John, Lord Chatham, from whom it passed by descent. This chair has many well carved features including the Royal Arms, the names 'Victory' and 'Trafalgar', drapery centred by a ship's rudder, oak leaves and acorns, dolphins, anchors and cannon arm rests, no doubt representing the twenty-four pounders used on board H.M.S. *Victory*. The ship was repaired in Chatham in 1806 and it was probably at that time that the oak used for this chair was stripped out. It seems fitting that for such an historical British souvenir oak should have been used, the very stuff of our countryside!

Glass

———⦿———

WE were told at school that the window panes were liquid; that glass is a liquid. But the rock solid diamonds of cut glass and engraved crystal at Mallett's look static to me. Equally, simpler forms of blown or shaped glass have all the appearance of ancient polished rock crystal, which of course is exactly what early glass makers aimed to achieve.

The glass department at Mallett's is only ten years old though the firm has always dealt in good pieces from time to time. Most of the objects are divided between drinking glasses with associated decanters, bowls, jugs, etc and lighting fixtures, chandeliers, wall lights, candelabra and so forth.

The first of my selection of representative highlights is a very beautiful pair of early eighteenth century candelabra (fig. 414). These very rare objects, made in England between 1710 and 1720, have five branches stemming from honeycomb moulded bowls with gilt metal receivers. The domed feet have trailed chain decoration and are held within an ormolu moulding. The beautiful stems have annulated knops with tears. No other perfect examples of this form are known though related all-glass four arm candelabra are in the Victoria and Albert Museum and the Corning Museum of Glass, New York State.

Superb Dutch engraved goblets include a garniture of three by Jacob Sang (fig. 416). Consisting of a large covered goblet and a pair of smaller ones, the first commemorates the silver wedding of Jan Westendorp and Sara van Wijlick on 7th February 1759. The two Kraamvrouw goblets commemorate the birth of their grandchild. The three pieces are beautifully engraved with the wedding church, bedside celebrations at the birth and inscriptions in addition to floral borders on the covers. The goblets themselves are sophisticated and elegant in shape.

Another rare piece from England is a glass epergne, or sweetmeat tree of circa 1760 (fig. 417). This extraordinary and charming object is topped with a panel moulded ogee-shaped bowl with three tiers of four scroll branches, hung with graduated baskets. Epergnes of silver and occasionally porcelain

414
Perhaps unique survivors of early English glass candelabra is this pair, each with five branches and with gilt metal bases and receivers where the arms join the stems. Circa 1715.

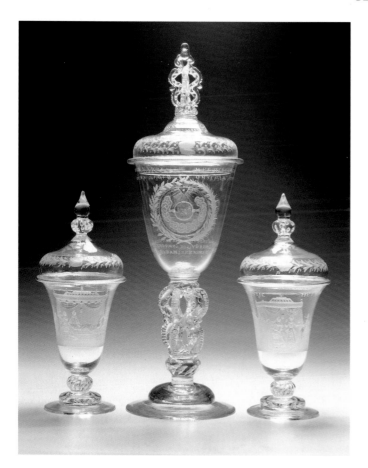

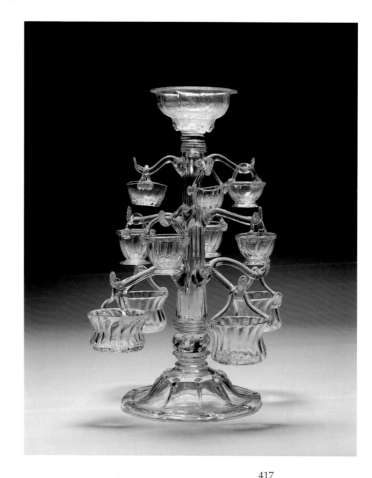

416

A superb garniture of three Dutch engraved goblets by Jacob Sang, the tallest commemorating a silver wedding in 1759.

417

An extremely rare and charming English glass epergne of about 1760.

are found from time to time but ones of glass are rare and these are usually later in date and of cut glass. This one was acquired by the Huntington Museum, Los Angeles. It had previously been at Brockenhurst Park, Hampshire.

Chandeliers are the grandest of all glass objects, always a symbol of brilliance and an emblem of luxury. Amongst some magnificent English examples that we have been lucky to handle is a glorious one of the late eighteenth century (fig. 415). Ormolu mounted, this cut glass chandelier has twelve arms, six upward pointing and six of 'S' form, all cut with six sides, as was the style in 1790. The pans have notched tips beneath cylindrical nozzles and the shallow receiver bowl is surrounded by an ormolu band, matching the upper canopy, above which is an ormolu florette. The stem contains a magnificent urn and the chandelier is dressed overall with pear shaped drops. It came from Braco Castle, Perthshire, formerly the seat of the Graham family, Earls of Montrose. The total height is 5 ft 9 in. Two rare Irish mirrors (figs 418 and 419) each one with a suspended chandelier before it are small, 25½ in. high. They have plain oval mirror plates framed within a border of diamond cut glass backed with green foil in the case of one, and blue on the other which also has alternating gilt fluted triglyphs. In the case of the green bordered mirror, the cut glass chandelier is lined in the stem and receiver bowl with internal gilding.

Fig. 420 shows a very grand pair of Regency cut glass claret jugs bearing the crest of the 11th Duke of Norfolk. In style these are similar to a well known suite in the Royal Collection, but claret jugs, with handles, in this pattern are previously unrecorded. In 1806 the Prince of Wales made a civic

415

An exceptional late eighteenth century twelve light cut glass chandelier with ormolu mounts.

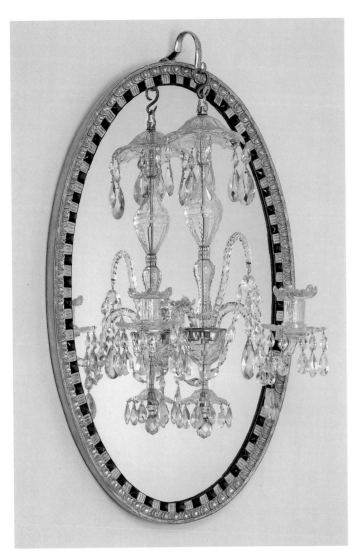

418 and 419

Two very fine Irish mirrors with suspended cut glass chandeliers, of about 1780.

420

A fine pair of early nineteenth century cut glass claret jugs, similar to a suite of glass made for the Prince Regent in 1806.

421

*A collection of
nineteenth century
coloured glass
decanters, hyacinth
vases, fairy lights
and an acorn vase.*

visit to Liverpool. In honour of this occasion the Mayor of Liverpool ordered
a superb suite of glass from the nearby firm of Perrin, Geddes and Co. of
Bank Quay, Warrington. This suite was engraved with the Liverpool
Corporation Crest. A contemporary commentator wrote, 'The Prince of
Wales had greatly admired the Glasses that were procured for his table at
the dinner and that he had requested the Mayor to order him a few dozen
Glasses of the same sort…' The Corporation graciously complied, but were
probably rather dismayed when the total sum came to £1,306 8s. The final
order consisted of 12 decanters, 36 coolers, 6 carafes or water jugs, 10 dozen
claret glasses, 4 dozen wine glasses, 6 dozen port glasses, 4 dozen clarets and
3 dozen goblets. The majority of this suite is still in Windsor Castle, although
a few examples have 'escaped' from the Royal collection and a decanter and
glass may be seen in the Victoria & Albert Museum in London. Our claret
jugs were likewise made in Warrington, circa 1810. The engraved crest of
the Howard family presumably relates in this instance to the 11th Duke of
Norfolk.

On a different level of glass making is a very decorative collection of
coloured wine decanters, hyacinth vases, fairy lights and an acorn vase
(fig. 421). During the nineteenth century a wide range of colours was

developed for use in glass making. Most of these items are in glass of solid colour but the green and red decanters are both made of cased glass which has been cut through to show the clear glass underneath.

Later chandeliers are represented by a magnificent one of twenty lights (fig. 422). Made by the firm of Perry and Co. in about 1845, this has two tiers of ten lights surmounted by ten spires. The chandelier is dressed overall with festoons of button drops and hung with elongated pear drops. The column is made up of baluster shaped pieces, all step cut, as is the bowl. The top and bottom canopies have scalloped rims. Perry and Co. (formerly Perry & Parker) was the largest and most successful (both commercially and artistically) of all the London chandelier makers up to the 1860s. This one is especially elegant.

The highlight of an interesting exhibition that included sulphides was a rare pair of crystal vases with polychrome decoration (fig. 423). These are cut glass vases with gilt bronze mounts and with internal enamel floral groups fired on a 24ct gold base. Though attributed to Baccarat they were most probably made at the Voneche factory in France and cut and mounted by L'Escalier de Cristal, Paris in about 1830. They are 14 in. high.

A tour de force of glassmaking is a massive Baccarat candelabrum with twenty-four lights (fig. 424). It is identical to one in the Baccarat museum in Lorraine, made by that company for the International Exhibition in Paris in 1878. In 1880 Baccarat opened a showroom in Bombay and this candelabrum (marked number 6) must have been a principal exhibit. It was subsequently adapted for electricity, but is shown here with candles. It stands to a maximum height of 7 ft 3½ in.

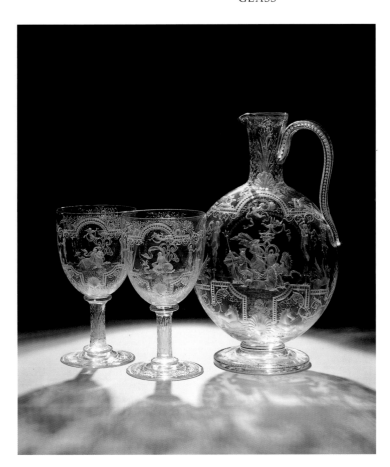

425

A late nineteenth century claret jug and two goblets magnificently engraved by Paul Oppitz who came to London from Prague in 1843.

424

A massive cut glass candelabrum with twenty branches made at the Baccarat factory in France in about 1878.

Another noteworthy exhibition item, this time engraved glass, is a superb ensemble consisting of a claret jug and two goblets by Paul Oppitz (fig. 425). This remarkable engraver was born near Prague in 1827 and emigrated to England in 1843. He eventually settled in Clapham, London. A vase commissioned from him by Alderman Copeland was exhibited in Vienna in 1873 and is now in the Victoria and Albert Museum. The pieces illustrated, of circa 1885, are superbly engraved with Neptune, mermaids and seahorses amidst Bérainesque strapwork, shells and scrolling forms.

The ultimate in glass works, in terms of English furniture history, are indeed sizeable pieces of furniture. Cut glass cabinets, tables and chairs were made by the firm of F. and C. Osler, founded in Birmingham in 1807. In 1848 Prince Albert commissioned a pair of glass candelabra ten feet high as a present for Queen Victoria and these are still at Osborne House on the Isle of Wight. The fame of Osler was such that the company was invited to make and install a crystal fountain around twenty feet high which was the centrepiece of the Great Exhibition of 1851. The firm was one of England's leading chandelier makers and made other lighting fittings as well as substantial pieces of furniture, especially for their princely clients in India. As well as premises in Birmingham. Osler had large showrooms in London's Oxford Street, designed by Owen Jones, and showrooms in Calcutta, then the capital of India. A surviving visitor's book for the London showrooms demonstrates that a trip to Osler's was one of the sights of London that no wealthy or Royal personage visiting London would miss. The company had skilled metalworkers enabling them to provide their own structures and ormolu mounts. One of the more remarkable pieces which

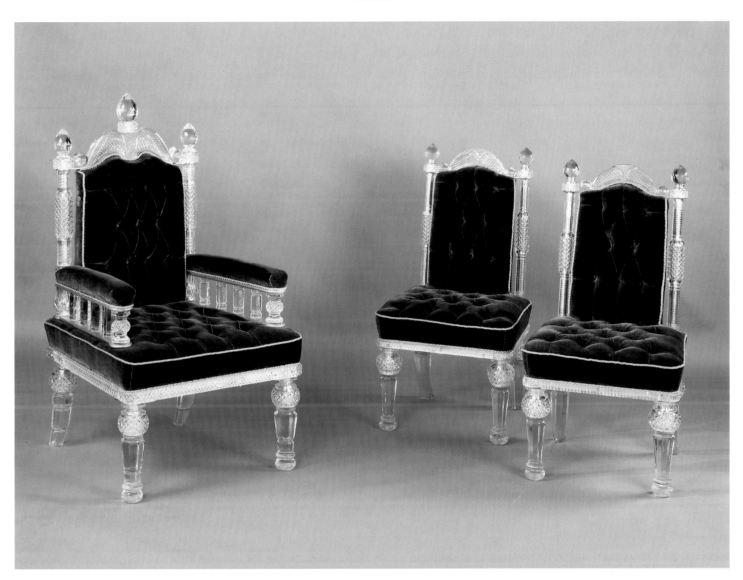

427
Also by Osler are three glass throne chairs, the cut glass fitted to invisible metal and wood frames.

we have had is a colossal cut glass sideboard, the design numbered and illustrated in Osler's pattern book of 1887 (fig. 426). 10 ft high and 6 ft 4 in. wide, the design shows elements of Islamic ornament, a feature also prevalent in contemporary cabinetmaking. Lord Leighton had a Moorish room while Liberty's also introduced such Eastern as well as Japanese motifs. Osler's Calcutta showrooms were patronised by many of the late nineteenth century Muslim rulers of the North Indian Princely States.

A further remarkable example of Osler's furniture is a set of three chairs, an armchair and two side chairs (fig. 427). Several versions of this form were made, with slight differences in detailing. Despite their fragile appearance they are in fact remarkably strong being built around a metal and wood frame that supports the velvet upholstery. Furthermore glass in large pieces is very strong (and indeed heavy), though cut decoration is of course prone to chipping. Such furniture naturally had tremendous allure for patrons in hot countries for not only was it spectacular but it looked fresh as ice, it did not warp, was not spoiled by heat and nor was it prone to be eaten by local insects. It will surely last longer than walnut furniture, which is especially desirable to woodworm.

426
Perhaps the ultimate in both furniture and glass, a colossal sideboard in cut glass by Osler. English, circa 1887.

The Nineteenth Century

THE Regency and Empire periods in England and France respectively carried into the nineteenth century an extended and more dramatic form of neo-classicism that had been initiated some fifty years earlier. In England it was still Georgian by name and essentially Georgian by nature. From the late 1830s however (Queen Victoria was crowned in 1837) it seems that furniture history takes a pattern of a long line of revivals and pastiches. There is much truth in this but there was also colossal development in every facet of the arts with a distinctive searching for new forms, and a corresponding range of inventive interpretations. In the end a great variety of soundly based designs and techniques with world-wide origins were developed, sometimes to the highest degree of quality. With the development of precise tools and machinery extraordinary feats were possible and these were demonstrated at the prestigious Great Exhibition of 1851. Sceptical of the merits of these mechanical developments the philosophies of William Morris and the Arts and Crafts movement provided a different angle to the concept of what should be considered of artistic value and what should not.

My selection of interesting nineteenth century things which have passed through Mallett's (several are included in other sections) illustrates a wide range of thinking in a period of great prosperity in British history and reflects an all-embracing inheritance of the past, as well as the benefits of broad territorial possessions.

Much English furniture retained key elements of the most successful features of previous styles, with added 'improvements'. While a walnut kidney shaped kneehole desk (fig. 429) is made in a vaguely Queen Anne tradition, even with late seventeenth century drop handles, and kingwood crossbanding around the drawer fronts reflecting later eighteenth century, the form itself is original and hugely pleasing. It was made in about 1850. On the reverse side it has bookshelves.

A magnificent boulle bureau plat (fig. 430) made in England by Thomas

428

In a corner at Bourdon House are three pieces of mid-nineteenth century oak furniture in a gothic style, neo-mediaeval in ornament but entirely 'Georgian' in proportion.

429
A kidney shaped desk of about 1850 is of an entirely original form, though the use of walnut and the cabinetmaking are historical.

Parker in about 1830 is an even more directly inspired revival of an old and much admired form, that hardly ever fell from fashion. Edward Holmes Baldock, a furniture dealer and cabinetmaker supplied a superb Louis XIV bureau plat to the 5th Duke of Buccleuch. Now at Boughton House this writing table is very close in design to our illustrated nineteenth century version. It has to be assumed that Thomas Parker who made furniture of

430
A magnificent Louis XIV revival boulle writing table by Thomas Parker, circa 1830, closely modelled on a specific seventeenth century bureau plat.

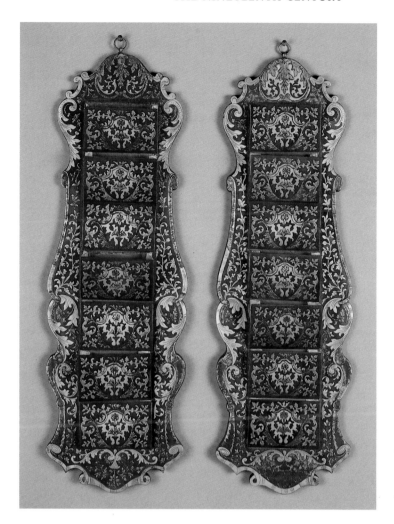

431

A pair of French aide-memoires with seven daily pockets for visiting cards or notes.

this style and of very high quality for George IV had access to the one that Baldock had acquired for the Duke. The bureau plat is decorated with fine marquetry of brass and red lined tortoiseshell and enriched with gilt bronze mounts including deep acanthus sabots on the cabriole legs, and male and female masks on either side of the table. Smaller examples of the boulle technique, but made to an exceptionally tight and rich pattern are a pair of aide-memoires of circa 1840 (fig. 431). These small wall brackets have, in each case, seven folding pockets for visiting cards. Kingwood is inlaid with brass and pewter in a dense pattern of foliate arabesques and scrolls.

Three small letterboxes (fig. 433) are each made of oak and date from the second half of the nineteenth century. These miniature pillar boxes would have been placed in the entrance hall to gather household letters ready for the postman and the collection times were noted on the front of each. A small drawer in the base of two of these would have been for postage stamps. An enamelled or brass flap in the opening slot is engraved with the word 'Letters'. The smaller box bears the supplier's name, H. Rodriguez, 42 Piccadilly, London with the design registration mark.

The frame of a high backed armchair (fig. 436) made in about 1860 in France, in the manner of A. M. E. Fournier is carved to simulate rope with knots and loops, and gilded. While we have seen a number of stools in this amusing trompe l'oeil pattern we have only seen this one large chair.

432
The epitome of fine Victorian craftsmanship this card table designed by J. D. Crace in 1886 combines both gothic and Renaissance motifs, and fine carving and marquetry.

Presumably others were made but the form is rare. This was acquired by the Metropolitan Museum of Art, New York.

Neo-gothic furniture was just one of the decorative fantasies of the eighteenth century rococo period and of course Horace Walpole's Strawberry Hill decorations epitomised the most fanciful forms of this taste. Curiously, although the motifs harked back to mediaeval architecture, in the eighteenth century they were applied to Georgian classical proportions as superficial decorative features. In the nineteenth century there was a more radical revival of mediaevalism but the traditional compromises continued. A splendid large partners' desk of circa 1840 (fig. 434) is of oak with inset panels of pollard oak. The paired gothic arches are placed between cluster columns. Apart from these features, the desk retains the proportions of an eighteenth century mahogany one. The fine colour is also more characteristic of Georgian furniture than either early oak furniture or later Victorian revivals of mediaeval style furniture. More gothic furniture of oak is shown in fig. 428 on page 330. In this corner at Bourdon House is a desk and bookcase and also a chair with gothic carving in the back and on the legs.

433
Three Victorian miniature pillar boxes of oak were used for the collection of letters in the entrance hall.

434
A magnificent early Victorian partners' desk of oak with gothic features adapted to Georgian proportions.

435

Very elegant and highly sophisticated in design and workmanship, this table was designed by Owen Jones and made by Jackson and Graham in about 1870.

One of the most original and fascinating suppliers of fine quality furniture in the middle of the nineteenth century was the firm of J. G. Crace and Son. A folding card table (fig. 432) was made by Crace in 1867 for Mr William Gibbs of Tyntesfield House, Wraxhall, Somerset. The pair to this table, now in the Cecil Higgins Art Gallery and Museum, Bedford, was designed by John Diblee Crace in 1886. The family firm had previously been involved with the redecoration of Carlton House and the Brighton Pavilion for the Prince Regent and subsequently undertook work at the Great Exhibition. The illustrated card table displays the strong influence of A. W. N. Pugin, with gothic revival elements in the design but also incorporates elements of neo-Renaissance that characterised the Crace firm. Predominantly burr walnut the table is inlaid with marquetry bands, roundels and cartouches resembling mediaeval mosaic work while some carved mouldings and pendants, together with an elaborate gothic brass stretcher enriched with glass cabochons add richness. The interior is lined in crimson baize with the original gilt tooled leather borders. Every detail was conceived and made to the highest standards of nineteenth century craftsmanship.

Much less ornate in appearance but equally beautifully made is a marquetry writing table of about 1870 (fig. 435). Designed by Owen Jones and made by Jackson and Graham, this elegant Victorian table with a leather top has bowed ends and stands on turned legs linked by a bowed cross-frame stretcher. Every surface is intricately and richly inlaid with marquetry of precious woods and ivory, the top and frieze being in calamander and rosewood. The marquetry takes the form of complex geometric patterns linking hexagonal patterns. There is a hidden drawer in the frieze. While the

436

A very unusual carved giltwood armchair in the form of a continuous rope with knots. French, circa 1860.

437

A large glass table made by Baccarat in France circa 1890, constructed around a silver plated frame, with a mirrored top and with many fitted sections of moulded glass. One other was made, now in the Corning Museum of Glass, New York.

438

Heavier and more 'Jacobean' than fig. 435 this table attributed to George Trollope combines superb qualities of carving, veneering, marquetry and metalwork.

table is simple in overall line and shape, on closer examination it exudes great quality through extreme attention to detail.

Another remarkable nineteenth century table is shown in fig. 438. Also with bowed ends but heavier and more sculptural in appearance this is of burr walnut with a veneered top surface, perhaps for a library. An almost identical table in the Victoria and Albert Museum has part of a label indicating 'G. Trollo' and it is assumed that both tables were made by George Trollope and Sons who exhibited at the Paris International Exhibition of 1867. Typical of mid-Victorian eclectic taste, the design incorporates a mixture of Renaissance and gothic decoration, here carried out in very high quality. The top and frieze are finely inlaid with scrolls, leaves, husks and overlapping circles, in boxwood and ebony and each is banded with cast brass mouldings. Carved end supports centred by bosses on lozenge shapes, are flanked by pillars with gothic stringing and gilt brass Corinthian capitals. A turned stretcher is inlaid in similar fashion and centred by a fluted panel.

Showmanship was often a feature of great furniture. The Baccarat glass table in fig. 437 is certainly an example of this, as is the Osler glass furniture discussed on page 327, but traditional suppliers of wood, marquetry and ormolu also conceived spectacular pieces, as we have seen.

A magnificent octagonal table attributed to Jackson and Graham and a design of Owen Jones again displays a great variety of techniques and design motifs including Moorish patterns. English, circa 1880.

A magnificent late nineteenth century amboyna wood and ivory inlaid octagonal centre table (fig. 439) is attributed to Jackson & Graham and to a design by Owen Jones who, with others of the mid-nineteenth century introduced a revival of Moorish patterns in conjunction with the familiar Renaissance revival and gothic motifs. His publication *Plans, Elevations, Sections and details of the Alhambra, 1836–45 and later The Grammar of Ornament* are testimony to the development of such decoration. From the early 1850s Owen Jones had a link with the luxury cabinetmakers Jackson and Graham, (later to merge with Collinson and Locke) whose Oxford Street premises he redesigned in 1869. This table combines the use of warm coloured burr veneers of amboyna with ebonised wood in the base. Likewise there is a further combination of brass mouldings, carving on the legs and feet, and intricate inlay on the top. This marquetry is in the form of a deep border made up of lines and bands of plain and chequer patterns, berried leaves, Greek key and stylised palmette spandrels issuing from chequered roundels. The top is 4 ft 10 in. wide.

Some of these fine touchstones of nineteenth century cabinetmaking show every bit as much originality, richness of design and quality of workmanship as top quality Georgian furniture and it is good that fine examples have come to light in recent decades after a long period of neglect.

Royal Visitors

'B Y Appointment to Queen Mary' was a distinction granted to Major Goodland, the then Chairman of the firm in 1945 and it was permitted for use long after her death. It was a greatly valued hallmark of approval since Queen Mary was renowned as a connoisseur of the decorative arts. She visited the shop regularly (fig. 442). At 40 New Bond Street we had a charming but old-fashioned lift between the two floors. I believe Queen Mary was in it once with Francis Egerton when it got stuck. He said that that was in the days when you did not speak unless spoken to, and on that occasion the Queen did not speak. They were released quickly however. Queen Elizabeth II has not been to Mallett's in my time but when Her Majesty was married in 1947 there was a list of presents at Mallett, gifts to the then Princess Elizabeth and Prince Philip given by regimental and civil bodies, presumably for their new home at Clarence House. David Nickerson used to tell of an occasion after she had become Queen. He was relatively a new boy in the business and had the fun of taking two friends, Fred Astaire and Bob Hope, around the shop. The experience took on a further dimension when as the two entertainers took David's arms and were doing two or three dance steps, who should walk into the room but Her Majesty. Apparently she showed great delight in seeing these other visitors to Mallett's.

Her Majesty Queen Elizabeth the Queen Mother has visited Mallett's on a number of occasions and I'm told that in the old days she loved to buy things, though fastidious equerries in the background would be shaking their heads, hopefully discouraging our chairman from proposing such expenditure. The Queen Mother paid a visit to both shops and stayed to luncheon in July 1981 (see page 5). The Prince of Wales has also been a visitor to the two businesses (fig. 443). H.R.H. The Princess Margaret is known to have an artistic eye and indeed on visiting the shop saw a very fine ormolu and glass clock by Matthew Boulton, upon which she quickly remarked 'My sister has one like that, but hers has a name on it'. That one is

440

The splendid satinwood desk, seen here in our former premises, is believed to have been made for the Prince Regent, later George IV, for Carlton House. With silver handles bearing a crown, this form of writing table has since been known as a Carlton House desk.

442
*Queen Mary at
Mallett's in 1947.*

indeed signed on the dial. Our version, made at the same time as the original was made for King George III, was later acquired from Hotspur for the Courtauld Institute Galleries. Princess Margaret also showed a sense of fun on our stand at the Grosvenor House Fair, where she admired some Chinese wallpaper. Peter Maitland said he had seen some belonging to her mother displayed elsewhere, and obviously not used; he hinted that it was perhaps not required and might be available ...? Upon which Princess Margaret thanked him for her visit and left saying 'And I shall tell my mother of your impudent suggestion.'

441

*Included here are
a rare French
commode in red
lacquer and two
transitional chairs,
below a North
Italian neo-classical
mirror. On the
commode stand an
Apulian vase and
bronze figures of
Voltaire and
Rousseau.*

443
*H.R.H. The Prince
of Wales in 1982.*

444

Gawen Hamilton (1698–1737) A Conversation
Piece: The Du Cane and Boehm Family
Group, *circa 1734–5 extensively inscribed in an
early hand with biographies of the sitters on the
reverse of the canvas. Oil on canvas, 40 × 50 in.
It is contained in its magnificent original
giltwood frame carved with the arms of the
two families.*

The Gallery

———◆———

THIS anthology of treasures from the house of Mallett must come near to an end with a handful of paintings from a relatively new department, the picture gallery. Mallett always had a few paintings and a larger number of decorative pictures including watercolours and drawings. But for ten years now we have had separate showrooms in the Bond Street shop to display pictures of both importance and decorative charm and experts here who specialise in this department. While Christopher Wood was with us, we naturally remained focussed on the area of his special expertise, fine Victorian pictures. More recently the scope has been wider and we pursue eclectic interests, as we do in the other parts of the business, dealing in anything we feel is truly interesting and of excellent quality.

Amongst some early decorative pictures painted on vellum we have had an exceptional pair (one shown in fig. 445), which were attributed to the seventeenth century artist Octavius Montfort. The miniaturist style of the painting, with the best characteristics of early vellum book illumination, gives these compact flower groups a special quality of richness with softness. They were approximately 18 in. by 15 in.

The most important eighteenth century painting that we have been fortunate to handle is a great work by the Scottish born artist Gawen Hamilton (fig. 444). In its superb original frame, this is a conversation piece, *The Du Cane and Boehm Family Group*, with portraits of sixteen members of the two families shown in a grand interior. Painted in oils on canvas, this is the finest and best preserved work by Gawen Hamilton who was Hogarth's contemporary and rival, and believed by some in his day to be a superior painter. The picture commemorates a union between these distinguished Huguenot families, each of which was represented by Directors of the Bank of England. Considerable research has been carried out by Elizabeth Einberg to identify members of the families, including those represented on the wall behind, and complex family trees have identified various relationships. It is enough to say here that by any account

446
*Ranelagh Barrett
(active 1737–d.1768)*
Four of Sir Robert
Walpole's Hounds
in a Landscape.
*Signed. Oil on
canvas, 60 × 94 in.*

this is an outstanding conversation piece and a tour de force of portrait painting. The frame also appeals to our furniture instinct of course; it too is in wonderful condition, the magnificent carving retaining its original gilding. The armorial achievements of the couple, Boehm impaling Du Cane, is not only carved on the frame but echoed in the plasterwork depicted over the central bust on the back wall. The picture was probably commissioned by Richard Du Cane to celebrate his daughter Jane's good marriage to Charles Boehm. This painting was acquired by the Tate Gallery, London.

A very large and charming painting, *Four Hounds in a Landscape* (fig. 446) is by Ranelagh Barrett (active 1737–1768) after John Wootton. This shows four of Sir Robert Walpole's hounds, and is signed 'R. Barrett'. Sir Robert Walpole was England's first Prime Minister and the builder of one of the grandest Paladian Houses, Houghton Hall, Norfolk, where he amassed a very important collection of paintings and furniture. His grandson however was unfortunately forced to sell all the paintings to Catherine the Great of Russia, including the original of this hound picture, by Wootton, though this original frame remained in the house. Ranelagh Barrett painted several canvases after lost originals including this charming picture. Each of the dogs have great character and must have been favourites of the Prime Minister.

445
*One of a pair of
flower pictures,
painted on vellum
attributed to
Octavius Montfort.*

Nineteenth century pictures

We were fortunate to be the owners for a short while of a remarkable painting by Tissot (Jacques Joseph Tissot 1836–1902) entitled *Chrysanthemums* (fig. 447). The reappearance of this picture was exciting as it was one of the artist's best paintings that he sent for exhibition at the Grosvenor Gallery in 1877. It is the largest and most spectacular of Tissot's pictures of women in conservatories, the unknown lady being posed in a fascinating and slightly mysterious manner and in perfect combination with a stunning background of flowers. The picture was acquired by The Sterling and Francine Clark Institute, Williamstown.

Amongst Victorian watercolours that we have seen a great favourite of mine was *The Old Mews Garden, Chelsea Hospital* by Helen Allingham, signed and dated 1870 (fig. 450). The watercolour was exhibited in 1877 and a letter attached to the back from Albert Goodwin says that it was 'the best thing in the exhibition'. Helen Allingham was marvellous at recording the warm atmosphere of old Kentish cottages and their homely gardens. Here in larger scale than usual she has captured the dignity of the revered old pensioners and two pretty girls in the garden of Charles II's Royal Hospital for elderly soldiers, which was designed by Sir Christopher Wren.

Sir Edward Burne-Jones was the most celebrated pre-Raphaelite painter in England and the leader of the Aesthetic Movement. At that same Grosvenor Gallery Exhibition of 1877, mentioned above, he was singled out by Henry James and indeed became famous overnight. *Katie Lewis* (fig. 449) is a fascinating and unusual painting in his oeuvre, dated 1886. The child was the daughter of friends, she is shown lying outstretched on a sofa reading about St George and the dragon. She is dressed in dark green velvet and the entire background is restricted to a range of orange gold colours. Burne-Jones kept the picture for himself for many years but eventually presented it to Katie's parents, Sir George and Lady Lewis. Sir George was so overjoyed he could not express himself, we are told in a contemporary diary. Not painted as a commission, this is a most original child portrait, with no trace of Victorian sentimentality, but contains a special atmosphere of childish confidence and mood caught through an absorbing book.

The lovely *Portrait of Madame Roger-Jourdain* by Giovanni Boldini (fig. 448), signed and dated 1889, is amongst the painter's finest and was painted when he was at the height of his powers. It conveys much of the spirit of the belle époque with a love of fashion and chic. Madame Roger-Jourdain was a close friend of John Singer Sargent and both lived as neighbours with Boldini in Paris. Boldini was born in Italy but spent most of his working life in Paris where he enjoyed great success. This portrait which can be compared with Sargent's watercolour of Madame Roger-Jourdain (daringly shown lying on the grass) is a masterpiece and reflects Boldini's especially sensitive portraits of women, often excelling Sargent's in this respect.

A superb pair of large scale railway station pictures is shown in figs 451 and 452. These are by George Earl one of a family of painters known for painting dogs. 7 ft by 4 ft these canvases are full of fascinating late Victorian detail. Earl had exhibited two smaller versions in 1876 and 1877 at the Royal Academy but these larger and more elaborate versions date from 1893 and 1895. They are clearly his masterpieces and as pictures of the railway age, are comparable only to Frith's *Railway Station* of 1862, which is of very

447
Jacques Joseph Tissot (1836–1902) Chrysanthemums. *Signed. Oil on canvas, 46¾ × 30 in.*

448
Giovanni Boldini
(1842–1931)
Portrait of
Madame Roger-
Jourdain. *Signed*
and dated 1889.
Oil on canvas,
81 × 33 in.

449
Sir Edward Coley Burne-Jones, Bt., A.R.A. (1833–1898) Katie Lewis. *Signed with initials, inscribed 'EB-J to GBL' and dated 1886 on the painted book. Oil on canvas, 24 × 50 in.*

similar size. As in the Frith, Earl has used the stations and the trains as a backdrop to a continuous frieze of bustling figures, dogs, luggage, and sporting paraphernalia. *King's Cross, Going North* shows fashionable people setting off for holidays in Scotland while *Perth Station, Coming South* depicts their return. Both are full of anecdotal detail. The luggage is in itself of great interest, consisting of leather trunks, suitcases, gun cases, tennis racquets, golf clubs, fishing tackle and wicker baskets, with travelling rugs, newspapers and *The Graphic* magazine clearly visible. One of the gun cases is marked with a label from Bombay, indicating that its owner is a much-travelled sportsman. The numerous groups of dogs, mostly held by grooms, footmen, or station porters, are a notable feature of both pictures, and obviously very much an Earl family speciality. The composition of *Coming South* is dramatic, the train shed and the platform being set at an angle. This makes for an open scene, and enables us to see the bookstall, clock, and various notices on the wall of the platform to the right. Among the luggage are sporting trophies – stags' antlers, grouse, blackcock, and wicker baskets doubtless containing salmon, all testimony to successful sport in Scotland. There are numerous dogs. Earl may have used some of the same models

450
Helen Allingham The Old Men's Garden, Chelsea Hospital. *Signed and dated 1870. Watercolour, 15 × 24 in.*

451

George Earl (1824–1908) King's Cross Station, Going
North *signed and dated 1893. Oil on canvas, 48¼ × 84 in.*

453

John William Waterhouse, RA (1849–1917) Flora and the
Zephyrs. *Signed and dated 1897. Oil on canvas, 44 × 81¼ in.*

452
George Earl
(1824–1908)
Perth Station,
Coming South.
Signed and dated
1895.
Oil on canvas,
48¼ × 84 in.

and costumes in both pictures, but has scattered them so carefully that it is very difficult to find the same person twice. There is a notice which reads 'No Smoking allowed in this Station' but several of the men seem to be smoking nonetheless. The clock shows the time as ten to four. Each carriage is separately labelled with its destination. These pictures are not only fascinating as social documents, they are perhaps the greatest pictures ever painted of the railway age at its zenith.

Another outstanding picture painted just over one hundred years ago is Waterhouse's *Flora and the Zephyrs*, signed and dated 'J. Waterhouse, 1897' (fig. 453). Again a large picture, 7 ft 9 in. long, this picture was exhibited by John William Waterhouse at the Royal Academy in 1898. The subject is derived from Ovid and portrays the moment when Zephyr, god of the wind, first sets eyes upon and falls in love with Flora as she gathers flowers in the fields with her maidens and children. He is accompanied by his winged companions and captures her by casting a garland of white flowers around her. The picture clearly harks back to Renaissance moods but with a uniquely original late-nineteenth century freshness that was greatly admired by the art critics of the day. It remains one of Waterhouse's greatest works.

It is fitting that this book, compiled to mark the end of the century, with an anthology of great furniture, objects and paintings, should come to a close with a work of 1897. I wonder what my successors at Mallett's will choose to write about in one hundred years time – I can't even conceive a millennium hence.

454

This needlework portrait of Charles I shows the king at his trial in 1649.
Measuring 13 × 11 in. it is derived from Edward Bower's painting in the
Royal Collection and is signed and dated 'Anna Skinner in the 69 year of her
age 1716.' It is said that the king sat in a chair of state but was not allowed
to wear a crown, only a tall hat and also that his beard turned grey at the
time of this terrible ordeal. Charles I was the earliest great collector in
England and in essence the founder of the Royal Collection.

455

These two remarkable gilt gesso tables of about 1720 have small differences in detail, but must have been conceived as a pair. One was illustrated in **Mallett's Great English Furniture**, *1991, and since then the second table was discovered. Both have recently been reacquired by Mallett. Of extraordinary grandeur and quality these tables epitomise an English culmination of taste and design in furniture, with Italian Renaissance strapwork patterns as interpreted by the French designer Jean Bérain and further modified and superbly carried out by English workshops of the early eighteenth century.*

456
Very similar to chairs at Osterley Park designed by Robert Adam and made by Linnell, this version and its pair is part of a further set, of which six from the Victoria and Albert Museum are on display at Kenwood, Hampstead. (See page 120.)

Index

457

A pair of Regency satinwood dwarf book cabinets.

458
*Twelve Regency
period tôle tea
canisters, numbered
and decorated with
chinoiseries.*

Truth did not come into the world naked.
It came clothed in forms and images.

St Philip